50 Capitalism Ideas
You Really
Need to Know

Jonathan Portes

greenfinch

Contents

Introduction

You can't understand capitalism without understanding economics. As an economist, of course I'd say that, and it's true. But it's also true that understanding economics gets you only part of the way to understanding capitalism. In writing this book, it's become clear to me that the story of capitalism is also that of history, of politics, of sociology and of culture – indeed, of modern society.

I've also realized that capitalism is full of contradictions, from the conjuring trick that is fiat money to the inherent instability of the financial system to the convenient fiction of supposedly efficient markets. As a result it is continually in crisis and its demise always appears imminent. Yet it is precisely those contradictions that make it dynamic and that have allowed it to evolve so successfully.

The purpose of this book isn't to convince you that capitalism is good or evil, or to predict the nature of the radical changes that will inevitably come over the next few decades. It's to explain the basic building blocks you need to understand how it works – money, banks, firms and markets. To describe the relationship between capitalism and other key historical and political concepts, like socialism and imperialism. To give the briefest of introductions to the contribution that some of the greatest thinkers of modern times made to our understanding of capitalist society – Adam Smith, John Maynard Keynes and most of all, paradoxically, Karl Marx. And to explore some of the less obvious connections, such as the analogy between capitalism and evolution and how capitalism is refracted through culture.

Inevitably I've left out far more than I could include, and there is plenty to disagree with and argue about. But I hope that there is enough here to convey the sheer breadth and importance of the topic, and to convince you that nobody who wants to understand how our society works can do so without thinking about how and why capitalism works.

Jonathan Portes

01 What is capitalism?

What do we mean by capitalism? How did the term originate? And how can any definition capture a concept that seems so amorphous and that is used to describe such a wide variety of countries and systems? Your answers to this may be quite revealing about your own political and economic beliefs.

In 1991, not long after the fall of the Berlin Wall, the *Wall Street Journal,* 'local paper' for the small area of downtown New York that serves as the centre of the world's financial system, declared that 'We are all capitalists now.' It argued that capitalism had won two battles. First, the intellectual and theoretical argument: there was no serious, coherent philosophical alternative to organizing a modern economy. And, second, the political argument: almost every country in the world was now either a fully fledged capitalist economy, or had a government and society more or less committed to moving in that direction.

And, if asked, most of us would indeed say that capitalism is the defining principle of the global economy, and perhaps society as a whole, in the 21st century. But equally most of us, including many economists, would find it quite hard to say exactly what that means.

Defining capitalism

No one specific feature defines capitalism. Is it the private ownership of the means of production? Many have argued for this definition, but consider the case of China. Over the last two decades, this country has perhaps best exemplified the dynamic and transformative powers of capitalism, yet much of its economy still remains in state hands, and even within the private sector that does exist, state control and interference remains pervasive.

Perhaps capitalism can be defined as a system where markets, rather than state control, are used to balance supply and demand and to allocate resources, especially in key industries and sectors? But in the United Kingdom, which has as good a claim as anywhere to be the intellectual and practical birthplace of modern capitalism, both healthcare and primary and secondary education are provided free, with only a limited role for market forces of any kind.

Or does capitalism involve limiting direct government control over resources – the role of the state in taxing and spending? If that's the case, then why has government expenditure as a proportion of overall output expanded hugely over the 20th century in almost all developed countries? While that proportion has perhaps stabilized over the last two decades, it has not shrunk, and there seems no reason to expect it will do so in future. Moreover, as other countries develop, the size and scope of their government is typically increasing.

Or perhaps capitalism is an environment where businesses can choose what and how to produce, and consumers can choose what and how to consume, without government interference? Yet even in the USA, frequently regarded as an exemplar of a capitalist economy, regulations govern everything from the qualifications required to be a dance instructor to whether a vineyard in one state can ship wine to a drinker in another. Even those politicians and pressure groups who are most opposed to government programmes and taxes seem remarkably unconcerned about these limitations on the free market.

But despite all these contradictions, and despite the huge differences that remain between how economies work around the world, all these countries can fairly be described as 'capitalist'. So too can almost all the rest of the world (with the exception perhaps of North Korea and a few others that have chosen to cut themselves off from the global economy).

Capitalism and private ownership

So then, what does capitalism mean? 'Capitalism' itself is a rather odd name. Indeed, the 19th-century German economist Karl Marx, who is probably most closely associated with the concept, preferred to talk about the 'capitalistic mode of production'. For Marx, this was characterized by private ownership of the means of production, wage labour supplied by a worker class, and the 'surplus value' created by production accruing to the owners. We'll be learning much more of his ideas later.

Although private ownership is key, this definition in itself is inadequate. This book is not intended to be a dictionary, but it would be remiss not to attempt some kind of working definition of the system we'll be discussing throughout the following chapters. So in my view, capitalism embodies a system where private ownership of

A term like capitalism is incredibly slippery, because there's such a range of different kinds of market economies. Essentially, what we've been debating over ... is what percentage of a society should be left in the hands of a deregulated market system ... in general the debate is not between capitalism and not-capitalism, it's between what parts of the economy are not suitable to being decided by the profit motive.
Naomi Klein

much, if not all, of the means of production is central to the way the economy (and wider society) operates. Those private owners can, collectively and individually, decide what to produce in response to the economic (and sometimes social) incentives they

> Capitalism is the astounding belief that the most wickedest of men will do the most wickedest of things for the greatest good of everyone.
> John Maynard Keynes

face. Consequently, the structure of what is produced and consumed is determined to a large extent not by government, but by decisions, individual and collective, taken by shareholders, firm management and individuals, both as owners and consumers. In all of the countries described above, even China, this is now the case.

This undoubtedly sounds somewhat long-winded. But it is a very powerful concept. For good or ill, the interplay between demand and supply, between production and consumption, has proved to be an extremely powerful force in shaping the development of our societies for the last few centuries. Governments and other forces may intervene, often powerfully, to shape and constrain our choices, incentives and decisions, but ultimately it is private decisions, on both the demand and supply side, that matter most, and define capitalism.

The condensed idea
Private ownership of the means of production

02 Property and property rights

P roperty, the idea that inanimate objects and land 'belong' to somebody, is so inherent to our culture and language that for most of us it seems as if it must be part of human nature itself. Yet that is a hotly contested view, and indeed the way we now think about property is in fact a relatively recent invention.

Roman law did recognize property (if you were fortunate enough to be male and free, of course), but during the age of monarchical absolutism, it was seen as something derived first from God and then from the monarch, rather than from any moral right of the individual. God had given man dominion over nature, and appointed rulers to oversee us, so we 'enjoyed' our property on sufferance.

Property and theft

As the Marquis de Sade noted (prefiguring Proudhon's famous, if somewhat opaque, phrase 'property is theft'), it is very difficult to see that anyone has any inherent, natural claim to land ownership. Almost everywhere, we own land because we purchased or inherited it from someone who, at some point in the past, stole it or took it by force. For instance, many of the patterns of land ownership in the UK can be traced back to the invasion of 1066, when William the Conqueror handed it out to his Norman barons, or to the actions of monarchs in subsequent centuries rewarding or bribing their supporters.

> 'Tracing the right of property back to its source, one infallibly arrives at usurpation. However, theft is only punished because it violates the right of property; but this right is itself nothing in origin but theft.'
>
> *De Sade, L'Histoire de Juliette*

With the decline of religion-based views of property, a variety of different philosophical approaches to both explaining and justifying property ownership emerged. Anticipating Marx, 17th-century philosopher John Locke argued that value and hence property rights derived from labour input: so labourers had rights over the goods they produced, or over the land that they improved.

By contrast, Adam Smith had a more instrumental approach: while men had rights to life and liberty, property rights were created and maintained by government, and were primarily important because they served the purpose of promoting and facilitating trade and exchange. For theorists of capitalism, both positive and negative, property rights are essential: the right to own both physical capital and land, and therefore to capture the value of what is produced using that capital, is fundamental. Moreover, without the ability to transfer and exchange property and enter into contracts, there can be no markets and hence no market economy.

> Government has no other end, but the preservation of property
> John Locke

Property and the state

This means that the most important role of the state in a capitalist society is to define and protect property rights. In order to do this, the state needs at least to provide a legal system, to enforce the judgement of courts, and to have a monopoly of physical force to protect property. Even the most ardent advocates of limited government and unfettered capitalism therefore tend to believe that some form of government is required for these purposes.

But this raises questions for any absolutist conception of property rights. If government is to provide protections for property, then it needs a source of revenue, and the ability to coerce citizens into providing that revenue. That means taxation – yet what is taxation other than the right of government to force private citizens to hand over some portion of their property? Thus, the mechanisms needed to define and protect property rights inherently impose at least some limits on those rights. There is no absolute right to property, and there never has been in any actually existing human society.

Going beyond this, the Lockean view that the value of property, particularly of productive capital, derives solely from the efforts of its owner doesn't make a lot of sense in a modern economy. Today, government not only creates property and property rights in a

Property through history

Our concepts of who can and cannot own property, and what can constitute property, have changed considerably throughout history. Under Roman law, and right up until the 19th century, women (especially married women) had few or no property rights. At the same time, property rights over human beings – slavery, or to a more limited extent serfdom – were widely recognized. We now regard both of these concepts as entirely alien, and certainly not fundamental to the functioning of a capitalist economy, but this was not the case at the time.

'The right of the owner of a slave, to such slave, and to his increase, is the same, and as inviolable as, the right of any owner to any property whatever'.
Constitution of the State of Kentucky, 1850

Equally, there is no reason to believe that our views of property in future will remain unchanged. We regard it as natural and normal to own pets and farm animals today, yet they are clearly alive and sentient, albeit not necessarily intelligent. Will we think of this as an appropriate conception of property in a century from now?

negative sense (by providing a legal framework and protecting owners from theft and robbery) but in a positive sense, by providing a broader context in which capital can be productive. This can involve everything from transport networks to the education system and environmental protection, and once again, this framework needs to be financed and regulated.

'There is nobody in this country who got rich on their own. Nobody. You built a factory out there – good for you. But I want to be clear. You moved your goods to market on roads the rest of us paid for. You hired workers the rest of us paid to educate. You were safe in your factory because of police forces and fire forces that the rest of us paid for. You didn't have to worry that marauding bands would come and seize everything at your factory. Now look. You built a factory and it turned into something terrific or a great idea – God bless! Keep a hunk of it. But part of the underlying social contract is you take a hunk of that and pay forward for the next kid who comes along.'

Elizabeth Warren, US Senator

Property rights

If owning something means having the right to do what you want with it, then property rights are rarely unconstrained. I am free to buy any car I want, so long as it meets European pollution standards, and has approved government insurance. I can drive it anywhere I want, at least on public roads, but I need to have a driving licence and must stick within the speed limit. Even if I no longer want it, I can't dump it just anywhere, but have to dispose of it in an approved manner. It's mine, not yours or the state's, and the state will protect my rights over it. But how I can use it is quite tightly constrained – generally, if not always, for good reasons.

The web of rules and constraints that both define and restrict property rights is characteristic of a complex modern economy and society. Most capitalist economies attempt to resolve these tensions in part by imposing constitutional or political restrictions on arbitrary or confiscatory actions by governments that 'interfere' with property rights. But the idea of property rights as absolute rights is not philosophically or practically coherent in modern society.

The condensed idea
Property is a creation of government

03 The free market

For many people, capitalism and the 'free market' are synonymous. But what is a free market? The standard definition sees it as one where prices are determined by supply and demand, and that is free of government intervention, whether by state control of who can produce and what they can produce, or by government regulation.

Free markets seem to have strong attractions from both a philosophical and a practical economic perspective. On philosophical grounds, surely human freedom is maximized if we do not control what people can make, buy and sell, except where it is necessary to protect public safety or to stop them from harming others? On economic grounds, meanwhile, almost the first thing you learn in economics is that allowing markets to function will lead to the most efficient allocation of resources, and hence maximize overall welfare. This is known as the First Theorem of Welfare Economics.

> 'When workers get higher wages and better working conditions through the free market, when they get raises by firms competing with one another for the best workers, by workers competing with one another for the best jobs, those higher wages are at nobody's expense. The whole pie is bigger – there's more for the worker, but there's also more for the employer, the investor, the consumer, and even the tax collector. That's the way the free market system distributes the fruits of economic progress among all people.'
>
> *Milton Friedman*

Does this sound too good to be true? Maximize freedom, and we can also maximize welfare? The free market is a very powerful concept, but there really isn't any such thing – or at least, defining a free market as one without government intervention doesn't get us very far.

Unregulated markets? There's no such thing
We'd probably say that the market for books like this one is relatively free in most countries. Books are written by people like me and published by companies like Quercus. We negotiate a price for writing

the book; if I ask for too much, they find somebody else to write it, and if they offer too little I can find another publisher. Similarly, once it's published, you, the reader, decide whether to spend your money on this book, a different one, or indeed on something else altogether. The government doesn't tell Quercus how much they have to pay me, or how much they are allowed to charge you.

But it's not nearly as simple as that. First, there are some government restrictions on what I can write (although they mostly relate to things like pornography and violence, and if that's what you're after here, you're probably going to be disappointed). More importantly, however, the whole operation of the market depends crucially on government. Quercus and I sign a contract that governs how much they are promising to pay me and for what. That contract is interpreted by, and enforceable in, a court of law, where decisions are made by people who work for the government, interpreting and enforcing laws made by the government. And while you don't sign a contract with Quercus (or the bookseller) when you buy this book, there is still an implicit, and legally enforceable, contract between you and the bookstore. (If you find after getting home that all the pages after this one are blank, you have a right to your money back).

Nor, of course, could booksellers exist at all without a whole array of laws, such as those that prohibit shoplifting and illegal downloading. And, more broadly, the entire publishing industry could not exist without some form of copyright law and copyright enforcement.

None of this means that the market for books isn't a free market. It is, and supply and demand do determine what is produced and how much it sells for. But it does mean that the idea, advanced by some philosophers or more naive 'libertarian' economists, that free markets are somehow the natural state of affairs, and would survive with less or even no government, is incoherent. Free markets can't exist without government intervention – the question is what kind.

Necessary interventions

A more sophisticated definition that still preserves the essence of 'freedom from [direct] government intervention' would say that the role of government, or the state, is simply to provide a neutral legal framework to allow contracts to be enforced, allowing the maximum 'freedom' to producers and consumers. But even this approach quickly

Freedom is contingent on time and place, and the level of government intervention we regard as acceptable or necessary changes. In the Victorian era in the UK, there was heated debate about child labour – whether children should be allowed to work in factories, or sweep chimneys, and for how long.

> 'In the 19th century, a lot of people were against outlawing child labour, because to do so would be against the very foundations of a free market economy: "These children want to work, these people want to employ them... what is your problem? It's not as if anyone has kidnapped them..."'
> *Brian Eno*

Many of those who we now think of as being on the 'right side of history,' such as the great proponent of Free Trade John Bright, opposed laws to restrict child labour on the grounds that they interfered with the operation of the market.

runs into philosophical problems, because there's no such thing as a neutral legal framework. Gauging the appropriate degree of consumer protection (how and whether all contracts should be enforceable and so on) presents a host of difficult legal and sometimes political issues, and there is no one simple answer. Whether we like it or not, some government intervention is inevitable.

Indeed, sometimes government interference is necessary to allow particular markets to be 'free', in the sense of allowing prices to be set by supply and demand. There is a heated debate amongst economists as to whether, left unchecked, there is a natural tendency towards monopoly amongst a few, some or even most markets (see Chapter 7). But few deny that it is possible for monopolies to arise, either naturally or because one company succeeds in establishing a dominant position. And since a monopoly allows one company to set prices with a view to maximizing its own profits, then it is inimical to the idea of a free market. For this reason, most developed countries have some sort of legal mechanism to control or prevent monopolies arising in particular industries. In other words, we set up legal and bureaucratic mechanisms to intervene in the market, precisely in order to make it more free.

Does this mean there's no such thing as a free market? Not really. However free markets should not be defined by the absence of government intervention, but rather by the type of intervention and regulation, both in setting the overall legal framework and in saying what sorts of production and consumption are acceptable or not for any particular society. Freedom does not mean anarchy.

The condensed idea
Markets can't work in a vacuum

04 Capital

Capital actually has two somewhat different meanings, referring to physical and financial assets. While closely related, these are complementary rather than identical, and both are fundamental to capitalism. In fact, it could be argued that the combination of these two concepts of capital is precisely what makes capitalism possible.

In the physical sense, capital simply means a productive asset – something that is useful or valuable not because it is consumed directly, but because it can be used, usually in combination with human input, to produce something of value that can be sold and consumed. In practice, this could mean anything from a factory to a railway line to a computer. Recently, definitions of capital have expanded even beyond this to encompass intangible or non-physical assets like patents or software. But capital can also mean financial assets: not only money, but wealth held in any form, from bank accounts to equities to hedge funds, in such a way that it generates a return.

Capital accumulation

What links these two concepts together is the idea of capital accumulation, and the way in which one type of capital can facilitate the other. Suppose I own a shop. I buy goods, resell them at a profit, and spend that profit on my own consumption. The shop is a capital asset, in the physical sense, and I am using it to produce something: in other words, it is generating a return. But there is no dynamism or growth here. I'm not saving anything, and my business isn't growing. I own some capital, and you can call me self-employed, maybe even an entrepreneur, but I'm not really a capitalist yet.

But now, suppose I want to expand. I save some of the profit from my first shop, and perhaps borrow some money from the bank. I buy another shop and hire somebody else to work in it. My profits increase as a result, although of course now some of the return from the capital goes to pay interest on my bank loan.

At the moment, I own the entire business, but in order to expand further I need more financial capital to buy more physical capital. So I sell shares in what is now a chain of stores, and reinvest the proceeds. Now what was previously my own business is owned by the people who bought the shares. They own the profits produced by the business, which provide the return on the financial capital that they have invested. The process of expansion has created both physical and financial capital.

Savings and investment

Another way of looking at the interaction between physical and financial capital is to consider saving and investment. At first, I was consuming all my profit without saving anything, so I couldn't invest. One way of acquiring the financial capital to finance my investment was for me to save some of my profit. But after that, I started using other people's savings to finance investment – at first through bank loans, and later when they bought shares in my business. Savings represent financial capital, and finance, investment in physical capital. In a capitalist economy: you can't have one without the other.

'Natural' capital

The financial and physical assets we think of as capital have owners and market values, both in company balance sheets and in the national accounts we use to measure the size of the economy. In contrast environmental 'assets', such as forests, rivers and the air we breathe, usually don't have either, since they generally belong to the government or the public. As a consequence, it is often argued that we don't value them properly, and that some economic activities that appear to generate wealth might actually be making us worse off, if at the same time they degrade the environment. Hence the concept of 'natural capital', which includes all of these things, has been developed. In the UK, the government has established a Natural Capital Committee whose job it is to advise on how to value the environment and ensure it is managed efficiently and sustainably. In the long run, the objective is to integrate natural assets into the mainstream economic accounts. Putting a value on, for example, the landscape of the Himalayas is hard, but in a capitalist economy, where things that do not have a price are not valued, it may be the best way to ensure its preservation for future generations.

Is capital the same as wealth? Yes and no. Most of us build up our wealth through savings (either through our own efforts or, if we are lucky, through money inherited from our parents). That wealth is then invested, and those investments correspond to our ownership of capital. Such capital may be physical, such as houses, or financial, such as bank deposits or shares (either directly owned, or indirectly held through our pensions).

But not all wealth is directly productive. Houses, for example, are a special case. If you own your house and live in it, you might not think it is producing anything, but if you own a house and someone else lives in it and pays you rent, then it is producing something, even if you can't see it: you are in effect selling 'housing services' to the tenant. It's still the same house, however, so economists generally think of people who live in their own houses as owning capital, and consuming the 'housing services' provided by that house themselves, even though no money changes hands. In some countries this element of capital can be quite big. Property wealth in the UK is about one third of total wealth, and 'imputed rent' (the estimated value of housing services provided and consumed by owner-occupiers) may be worth as much as 10 per cent of the whole economy!

How do you value capital?

The key point here is that capital (by definition) is an input to producing things that people want to consume, rather than an output in itself. From an economic point of view, the value of a piece of physical capital should represent the value of the future profits to be made using that capital. But of course, this is not straightforward to calculate, and in practice it's much easier to calculate the value of financial assets, especially if they're traded on markets.

As manufacturing diminishes in economic importance, physical capital such as heavy machinery becomes less important overall. But that doesn't mean that capital no longer matters. 'Intangible' investments, such as software, research and development, branding and marketing, may be harder to see or measure, but they cost money and (if they are profitable) deliver a return. In the UK, businesses today invest more in intangibles than they do in traditional physical capital. Capital may change its form, but it is actually more important than ever.

What is everything in the world worth? One study – modestly entitled 'The Value of Everything' – made a valiant attempt to calculate the value of all capital assets in the world. This included stocks and bonds, property, infrastructure, land and forests, and everything else the researchers could put a rough number to. It came up with a value of $450 trillion dollars, equal to about $60,000 for each person in the world.

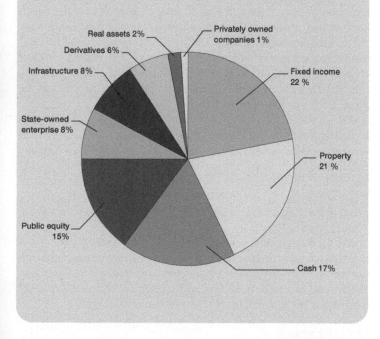

The condensed idea
Physical and financial assets

05 Labour and surplus value

Calling our economic system 'capitalism' is rather misleading. In fact, its defining feature is not so much the existence or even the importance of capital, but the relationship between capital on the one hand, and labour on the other – specifically, how the two are combined and who gets the benefits.

In the largely agrarian and rural society of the pre-industrial age, most people were either agricultural labourers on their own land or that of others, or self-employed. Labour (and land) were the main inputs into production, while the value of what was produced mostly went either to the people who produced it, or was creamed off (more or less forcibly) by the monarch, the aristocracy, the Church or by a state controlled by some combination of the three. Such was the system known as feudalism.

Things began to change, however, with the growth of trade and especially industrialization and mass production. Today, producing something usually needs both capital and labour. This book, for example, not only represents the fruit of my own personal labour, but also that of a number of other employees of the publishing company. It also required a computer to type it on, and (if it's a physical copy) a printing press. So, like most products, it incorporates both capital and labour inputs.

But the fundamental organizing principle of a capitalist economy is that this relationship is asymmetric. It is firms that provide and own the capital, and firms that sell the products and get the revenues. Workers simply receive a wage, while firms and their owners keep whatever is left after paying their workers and other costs.

Surplus value

Karl Marx's fundamental insight into the capitalist system was twofold. First, he realized that in a capitalist society, firm owners would seek to maximize their profit (which he called 'surplus value') by paying workers as little as possible. And second, he saw it was this surplus value, not paid out to the workers, that was therefore available to be reinvested in the firm (or in other firms), allowing more investment and more growth. As Marx saw it, then, capitalism would unleash two irresistible forces: the immiseration of workers, who would be paid just enough to keep them alive and healthy enough to work; and fierce competition between firms to create more surplus value and reinvest it, producing new and different goods and spurring an ever-growing economy. More and more of the benefits of this growth, however, would go to the owners of capital at the expense of the workers. And to ensure that workers did not use their bargaining power to push up wages, Marx hypothesized that capitalists would ensure wages were permanently depressed through the creation of a 'reserve army of the unemployed'.

Wages

By contrast, mainstream economics, which assumes that competitive markets determine prices, gave a rather different prediction. It argued that there is a market for labour as well: workers could choose to move from one firm to another to get a higher wage. In a competitive economy, therefore, firms wouldn't be able to get away with just paying subsistence wages, and the value created in production would be shared according to the 'marginal product' of capital and labour. Furthermore, because the marginal product of labour increases according to how much capital there is (a factory worker can produce more with a better machine, and I can produce more words faster with a computer than with a typewriter), wages should go up over time as the capital stock increases and workers become more productive. Indeed, John Maynard Keynes speculated that as capital accumulated faster than the labour force grew, the return on the ever-increasing capital stock would fall, and the proportion of value captured by workers would grow at the expense of capital owners – an effect he called the 'euthanasia of the rentier'.

So who was right? Marx's theory that capitalism would inevitably lead to subsistence or near-subsistence wages for workers, and that labour markets would not naturally push up wages as economies developed, has been comprehensively refuted. Of course, many would argue that labour did so 'well' in large part because of political and social developments that, in turn, owed much to Marx. Many capitalist societies modified themselves to deal with the challenge his ideas posed, giving rise to trade unions, social safety nets and a hugely expanded role for government. But it is worth noting that even in societies where these institutions are much less strong, and the existence of a 'reserve army' of labour seems much more plausible, labour markets still seem to drive wages. For example, despite the absence of a strong independent trade union movement, wages in urban parts of China have risen sharply in recent years, as workers demand (and, given the competition for their services, are able to obtain) a greater share of the value created by their labours.

Advantage capital

But past is not necessarily prologue. Many economists – even those, like me, who were brought up firmly in the neoclassical rather than the Marxist paradigm – are much less confident that workers, especially in developed economies, will do so well over the decades to come. As the influence of trade unions weakens and globalization expands, workers in developed countries face competition from lower-paid labour forces elsewhere – Marx's reserve army in another form.

> Labour was the first price, the original purchase – money that was paid for all things.
> It was not by gold or by silver, but by labour, that all wealth of the world was originally purchased.
> Adam Smith

And, looking forward, things look still worse. Technological progress and automation may mean that there is simply much less demand for today's low- and medium-skilled workers. Put another way, the marginal product of employed workers may fall, while that of capital (now meaning mostly software in one form or another) rises. More and more of the proceeds of future growth will go to the owners of capital, and less and less to workers. Marx may still have the last laugh.

The labour share

One of the most notable features of industrialized economies after the Second World War was that the 'labour share' remained relatively constant at about two thirds; that is, about two thirds of the total value created in the economy went to workers, and one third to capital (and hence its owners). So not Keynes' euthanasia of the rentier by any means, but workers, collectively, did capture their share of post-war growth. And while that doesn't mean that inequality didn't increase in many countries over the past few decades (within a constant labour share, some workers can do much better than others!) it is not consistent with Marx's hypothesis. But more recently, the labour share has been shrinking in many countries – a key question is whether this is just temporary or presages a much longer-term trend.

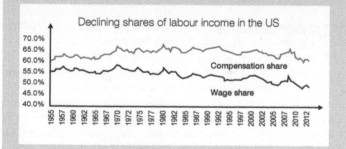

Declining shares of labour income in the US

The condensed idea
The struggle between capital and labour

06 Money

I t might seem obvious that money is fundamental to economics and hence to capitalism. But strangely, that isn't the case at all. Most of the key concepts of classical economics (supply and demand, free trade, comparative advantage, and so on) would still make perfect sense in a purely barter-driven economy, with no money as such. So what is the real function of money?

In the basic models we use to explain capitalist concepts, money doesn't matter – what matters is the relative supply and demand of goods, and hence their relative 'prices'. In practice, however, all real-world economies (even those that are largely or entirely state-controlled) have money of some sort. Money is deemed necessary because it has three related, but conceptually separate, purposes:

• **As a medium of exchange** A barter economy might be possible in theory, but while supply and demand may mean that this book is 'worth' three loaves of bread or one quarter of a new shirt, I can't in practice go to the supermarket with a few copies and hope to exchange them for my dinner. Any remotely sophisticated economy is based on indirect trade involving many different participants. Workers get food from the supermarket, the supermarket gets food from the farmers, the farmers get fertilizer from the factory, the factory is operated by the workers – and that's just one oversimplified example of this circular flow of goods and services. Money solves this problem, and enables this complex series of exchanges to work in practice.

• **As a unit of account** In order to measure the value of something, we need some form of common denominator. This allows us not only to trade directly for things at one single point in time, but also to write contracts, including ones that extend over a period of time, and that may include agreements over borrowing and debt. Since many of the most important economic transactions that we make are not one-offs (the terms and conditions of our employment, mortgages, and so on) a means of keeping track of what is owed is essential. And this is even more true for businesses.

• **As a store of value** Money can be saved so that people don't have to use it to purchase something immediately. They can instead smooth their purchases (and their consumption) over time. Of course, in order to be useful as such a store, money needs to hold its value relative to 'real' goods and services over time. If inflation (the rate of rising prices) is high and/or unpredictable, it can erode money's usefulness in this regard.

Money and gold

Originally, precious metals – especially gold and silver – seemed very well designed to serve all three purposes of money. Since they were in relatively fixed supply, they seemed to hold their value well across time (and place), so they worked well as a medium of exchange. Over time, for reasons of security and convenience, notes (representing ownership of a certain amount of gold or silver held in a bank) emerged. But at least in theory, the link to gold or silver remained: you could go to the bank and exchange your notes for the equivalent quantity of gold or silver. This was known as the 'gold standard'.

But it turned out that tying the supply of money to the supply of precious metals did not lead to stability: sudden changes in the availability of precious metals led to booms and then busts. Following

Evolving money

One of the classic academic papers on the origins and functions of money is R. A. Radford's 'The Economic Organization of a POW Camp,' written shortly after his release from Stalag VII, a Nazi prisoner-of-war camp. Radford's topic was the development of the camp's monetary system. Prisoners received a standard ration of cigarettes, to which most (but not all) were addicted. So, while cigarettes started out as a standard commodity for personal consumption, they soon became a currency, used by smokers and non-smokers alike for trading purposes. The prices of other goods, such as chocolate or soap, were quoted in cigarettes. Although cigarettes were not perfect as a store of value (they don't last indefinitely) they are otherwise well suited, since they are light and standardized. Radford's paper is still cited as an example of how money evolves 'naturally' from an economy that starts off by relying on barter for trade.

the conquest of South America, for example, the vast quantities of silver shipped back to finance the Spanish Empire's wars in Europe led to inflation, and (as the empire overspent) repeated defaults. Similarly, discoveries of gold in California and Australia in the 19th century led to a global boom, triggering first inflation, and then recession and deflation.

Moreover, private banks did not behave as if there was a fixed and stable quantity of gold at any one time. When the economy was booming they lent out more money than they held the gold to redeem, so that when the inevitable contraction came, the loans went bad, depositors wanted their money back and some banks failed. The gold standard exacerbated the bust just as it had exaggerated the boom. This culminated in the Great Depression of the 1930s, in which the gold standard played a central part. It meant that central banks (see Chapter 16) could not either expand the money supply or rescue the banking system. Countries like the United Kingdom, which left the gold standard relatively early, recovered much more quickly than those like the USA and France, which had stuck with it.

> In truth, the gold standard is already a barbarous relic.
> John Maynard Keynes

The fall of the gold standard

The experience of the Great Depression discredited the gold standard in the eyes of almost all economists, from John Maynard Keynes to Milton Friedman. And while the post-war Bretton Woods system did recreate a (watered-down) version of the gold standard, this did not survive the 1970s. No major or even minor economy remains on the gold standard today (although the fundamentalist Islamic State group recently released a video announcing that it would be minting gold coins – not a great recommendation).

So what gives money its value today, if not gold or some other real commodity? Modern currency is 'fiat' money – that is, money that has been declared to be money by fiat, or order, of the government. But this definition too turns out to be quite fuzzy. It is true that in some countries money is the only form of 'legal tender' (that is, a payment that governments, businesses or companies are obliged to accept). But in practice legal tender means little or nothing. For example, Bank of

England £20 notes are legal tender in England and Wales, but not in Scotland or Northern Ireland. Few people know this, and even fewer care, because it really doesn't matter; nobody in Scotland will refuse to accept an English £20 note as payment.

So, money can look all too much like a confidence trick. Fiat money, in either physical or digital form, is good for nothing and worth nothing in any practical sense – except insofar as other people believe in its worth. Money is only useful (in any of the three senses outlined above) because we all, collectively, agree that it can be used as such. Ironically, the proper functioning of a modern capitalist economy relies on this collective suspension of disbelief.

The condensed idea
It's money if you think it is

07 Monopoly

Nothing better exemplifies the tensions at the heart of the capitalist economic model than the interplay between competition and monopoly. In a capitalist society, competition is the force that leads to innovation, technological progress, increased productivity and growth. Monopoly, on the other hand, is widely held to lead to economic stagnation.

The desire to out-compete others provides the fundamental motivation for entrepreneurs and businesses to invest the necessary money and time in improving the production process. In contrast a monopolist, with a captive market and no competitive pressure, has no incentive to innovate and improve their product, and can charge the price that maximizes their own profits rather than that which creates wider economic benefits to society.

But too much competition, paradoxically, can also inhibit innovation. Profit gives an incentive to improve a product, or to invent a new one. But competition reduces profits and can sometimes eliminate them entirely, reducing these incentives. For many, perhaps most inventions, the main motivation is the prospect of having at least a temporary monopoly, and the profit-making opportunities that come with innovation.

Where do monopolies come from?

From an economic perspective, the main reason that monopolies emerge is the increasing returns to scale: that is, larger firms are likely to be more efficient. Competition will therefore mean that larger firms will drive smaller ones from the market. Moreover, creating a larger firm or factory requires more capital than a smaller one, but will deliver a higher return. So, over time, both capital and labour will eventually become increasingly concentrated in larger firms. A related reason is the network effect: the more connected a railway or telephone network is, for example, the more useful it is to the user, so in practice there is only room for one.

The second half of the 19th century seemed to bear this out. 'Robber baron' capitalists such as Andrew Carnegie in the steel industry, J. P. Morgan in banking and John D. Rockefeller in oil, created huge businesses that dominated the US economy. At its peak, Rockefeller's Standard Oil controlled 90 per cent of the country's oil market. As both Karl Marx and Adam Smith would probably have predicted, Rockefeller and others used both fair means (economies of scale and network effects arising from the size and reach of their businesses) and foul (price-fixing with competitors, predatory pricing and violent suppression of labour unions) to establish and maintain their market positions.

Anti-trust

Ultimately, however, the situation brought about a political reaction: in the late 19th and early 20th centuries, 'anti-trust' laws sought to break up monopolies and prohibit anti-competitive actions such as price-fixing. Standard Oil was broken up, and other monopolies such as railways were regulated. Implicitly, public policy recognized that unregulated capitalism does indeed have a natural tendency towards monopoly (at least in some industries), and that it is the role of government to inhibit this. The challenge is to do it without stifling the ability of businesses to innovate and grow.

In the 20th century, most countries sought to resolve these tensions in two ways. For most businesses, competition law restrained business practices that

> Like many businessmen of genius he learned that free competition was wasteful, monopoly efficient. And so he simply set about achieving that efficient monopoly.
>
> Mario Puzo, *The Godfather*

were thought to enable the establishment or perpetuation of an actual or effective monopoly (such as an 'oligopoly', when several businesses collude, either explicitly or implicitly, to raise prices or otherwise reduce competition). So price-fixing with competitors is usually illegal, and if a merger or takeover looks likely to significantly reduce competition it can be blocked. Meanwhile, businesses where monopoly was thought to be inevitable (so-called 'natural monopolies') were either nationalized or strictly regulated. Railways, telephone and electricity companies, for example, were either publicly owned, or faced strict rules on how much they could charge.

But the view that unregulated capitalism would always tend towards monopoly did not go unchallenged. Those with a more dynamic view pointed out that monopolies (especially regulated ones) would become sleepy and inefficient, ripe for challenge by more innovative competitors. They also argued that technological innovation could change the nature of some industries previously considered natural monopolies.

So in the late 1970s, again led by the United States, many countries began to deregulate key industries and privatize others. Where successful, this spurred innovation and led to gains for consumers. For example, airline deregulation, first in the US and then (more patchily) in Europe, was an obvious success. Privatization had more mixed results: in telecoms, where technological change genuinely made it much harder to create and sustain a monopoly, it has largely been successful; but in other industries, such as railways, less so. The consensus shifted from a view that constant and intrusive government intervention, direct and indirect, was required to ensure competition, to a more minimalist approach.

Monopoly and technology

In the first half of the 21st century, we may be approaching another turning point. The pace of technological progress has increased, and some argue this means that competition policy is both less necessary and less effective: government can't keep up, and doesn't really need to. For example, the US government spent considerable time and effort in the 1970s and 1980s pursuing court cases against IBM for its dominance of the mainframe computer market, but the situation was resolved when technological innovation meant that the PC market became far more important than the mainframe one. Similarly, Microsoft was found guilty of anti-competitive behaviour for attempting to establish a monopoly position for its Internet Explorer web browser, even as it was being overtaken by Google.

But there is a contrary view that new technology makes network effects (and hence competition policy) even more important. Google, Facebook and Amazon may not yet be the equivalent of Standard Oil or J. P. Morgan, but they clearly have some elements of monopoly power. And, as most theorists of capitalism would predict and expect, they are trying to preserve and expand their positions both by moving into new markets where they can leverage their existing dominance, and by using their control over our personal data to increase their profits. How should policy respond? We don't yet know, but it seems unlikely that a purely laissez-faire approach will be enough.

The condensed idea
Competition requires eternal vigilance

08 Comparative advantage

Comparative advantage, and the closely related concept of opportunity cost, are fundamental to understanding key features of modern economics, such as why specialization makes economies more efficient, why countries trade with each other, and why you should not always concentrate on the thing that you do best!

The concept of comparative advantage is sometimes abbreviated to the maxim that countries (or individuals, or firms) should specialize in doing things that they are 'good' at. But this risks confusing the concept of *comparative* advantage with that of *absolute* advantage. In fact, comparative advantage says that all countries will gain from trade, and that this is the case even if they are less efficient than the countries they are trading with, not just in some goods but in all goods.

Wine, cloth and the gains from trade

Economist David Ricardo, writing in 1817, set out a famous example in which Portugal is more efficient than England in producing both wine and cloth. Portugal has an absolute advantage in production of both goods, but despite this, Ricardo showed that both Portugal and England gain from trade. Without trade, England would need 220 man-years of labour to produce one unit of each, while Portugal would need a mere 170 years. But if England devotes all 220 man-years to producing cloth, it will produce 2.2 units; while if Portugal produces only wine with 170 man-years of labour, it will produce 2.15 units. If England then trades 1.1 unit of cloth for 1.075 units of wine, both countries will be able to consume more than one unit of each. Free trade has therefore benefited both countries. Even though Portugal has an absolute advantage in producing both wine and cloth,

Man-years of labour needed to produce one unit:		
Country	Cloth	Wine
England	100	120
Portugal	90	80

England is relatively better at producing cloth: it has a comparative advantage. Even after trade, England will still be poorer than Portugal. But England will be less poor with trade than without. Crucially, every country has a comparative advantage in producing something, and so all countries gain from free trade.

Comparative advantage also applies at the individual level. My wife may be better at me (that is, more efficient) at both economics and cooking. But I will have a comparative advantage at one or the other. And she has limited time. So we will both be better off if I concentrate on that one, and free up her time to concentrate on the other.

What determines comparative advantage?

For Ricardo, the crucial issue in determining comparative advantage was 'factor endowments' – how much land, labour and capital a country had available. So, a country that has lots of land and relatively few people might have a comparative advantage in agriculture, while one with lots of available capital might have one in manufacturing.

That's the theory. But does it work in practice? On the whole, it seems to. For example, Bangladesh, a relatively small, heavily populated country without much in the way of natural resources probably does not have an absolute advantage in producing anything at a global level. Anything made there could probably be made more efficiently somewhere else. But the country's abundance of unskilled labour gives it a comparative advantage in industrial sectors that use such labour, like textiles.

> Under a system of perfectly free commerce, each country naturally devotes its capital and labour to such employments as are most beneficial to each. This pursuit of individual advantage is admirably connected with the universal good of the whole.
> David Ricardo

So, when richer countries lowered or eliminated tariffs on textiles produced in Bangladesh, lots of textile factories sprang up there, and many workers (especially women) migrated from villages to the cities to work in them. This hasn't made Bangladesh rich – either as a country or as individuals – but the workers earn more than they did in the villages, and with that money the country can import food and other goods. Bangladesh remains one of the poorest countries in the world, but free(-ish) trade in textiles has helped it to achieve a dramatic reduction in poverty over the last decade.

Comparative advantage is more controversial when it comes to more advanced economies and products. The simple examples outlined above assume that comparative advantage is fixed, but while Portugal may have a permanent comparative advantage over England when it comes to wine, the sources of Silicon Valley or London's comparative advantages in software or investment banking are far less obvious, and may be related much more closely to the actions of government or firms (for example, as regards the education system or the legal and regulatory framework). This in turn makes it less obvious that free trade or free markets are always the right policy.

Comparative advantage is not fixed

In the 1950s and 1960s, in the aftermath of colonialism, 'infant industry' arguments were popular, with supporters suggesting that developing countries should give trade protection to particular industries until they could become globally competitive. However, countries that pursued this approach, including India and many in Africa and Latin America, were generally quite unsuccessful; it turned out that being 'protected' from free trade meant domestic industries never became efficient enough to compete globally.

But equally, this didn't mean that countries had to accept that comparative advantage was fixed. Many nations in East Asia, while maintaining fairly open trade policies, used a mixture of domestic regulation, subsidies and other government interventions to create comparative advantage in new industries. Japan did not achieve its current success in producing cars, or Korea its reputation for mobile phones, because of an inherent comparative advantage; rather, this was created by a combination of market pressures and government intervention.

> The idea of comparative advantage, like evolution via natural selection, is a concept that seems simple and compelling to those who understand it. Yet anyone who becomes involved in discussions of international trade beyond the narrow circle of academic economists quickly realizes that it must be, in some sense, a very difficult concept indeed.
> Paul Krugman

How do countries from France to Zambia create comparative advantage in today's global economy? Free trade and free markets are part of the answer, but so, too, are good institutions and infrastructure, the rule of law, high-quality education and, sometimes, direct government intervention. All of this involves hard work, but the fundamental insight, that everybody can be (relatively) good at something, and that you should concentrate on what you're (relatively) good at, still holds.

The condensed idea
Everyone is good at something

09 The invisible hand

The most striking metaphor in economics is Adam Smith's invisible hand. His insight was that, if markets work, then individuals rationally pursuing their own self-interest should, by doing so, maximize the overall value of what society as a whole produces. If this is true, then no collective planning, coordination or government intervention should be required. Smith introduced the concept in a pivotal passage of his 1776 treatise *The Wealth of Nations*:

> 'Every individual necessarily labours to render the annual revenue of the society as great as he can. He generally, indeed, neither intends to promote the public interest, nor knows how much he is promoting it. By preferring the support of domestic to that of foreign industry, he intends only his own security; and by directing that industry in such a manner as its produce may be of the greatest value, he intends only his own gain, and he is in this, as in many other cases, led by an invisible hand to promote an end which was no part of his intention ... By pursuing his own interest he frequently promotes that of the society more effectually than when he really intends to promote it. I have never known much good done by those who affected to trade for the public good.'

The price mechanism

But why would individuals pursuing their own self-interest serve the interests of society as a whole? The answer lies in the price mechanism. If markets are functioning properly, then individuals will maximize their own well-being by producing the most valuable products they can. And equally, as consumers, they will seek out and purchase the products that they find most valuable. Looking at the economy and society as a whole, the operation of supply and demand will mean that resources – both capital and labour – will be allocated where they are most valuable. The result will be the most efficient possible outcome.

This sounds like a nice theoretical argument when applied to supply and demand curves drawn in the classroom, but can it work in reality, which is surely far more complicated? In fact, while the

Feeding cities

Every day, more than 8 million people in London need to eat three meals. Very little of what they eat is produced in the city – in fact, it comes not just from all over the UK but all over the world. No single person or organization could comprehend, much less plan, everything that needs to happen to produce everything that we eat from beef to bananas, from biscuits to beer; and to transport those products, by plane, ship and truck to supermarkets and stores. And no-one does. In fact, almost none of it is 'planned' (at least, not centrally). Instead, it simply happens, as a result of the individual efforts of private companies, from international trading conglomerates to corner shops, each trying to make a profit. The invisible hand delivers something of a complexity and sophistication that planning never could.

'invisible hand' is far from perfect, it does do a better job of balancing demand or supply and satisfying individual and collective needs than planning ever could.

The First Fundamental Theorem

Smith came to his view intuitively, but a version of it has since been 'proved' mathematically by modern economists Kenneth Arrow and Gerard Debreu. The 'First Fundamental Theorem of Welfare Economics' states that if markets work, then the resulting outcome, the so-called 'competitive equilibrium', will be 'Pareto-efficient'. This means (in broad terms) that overall output will be maximized, and that no one can be made better off without someone else being made worse off. The simplicity and power of the invisible hand seem compelling both economically, politically and (for some) morally. And if an economy without government intervention is economically 'efficient', then surely there is no justification for intervention, which will only make matters worse?

But, as Smith recognized, the situation is considerably more complicated than that. Markets do not work at all without government

That is the lesson we draw from the economic history of the United States where again and again, government redesigned the US economy – shifting it into new growth directions. Yes, there was an Invisible Hand and lots of entrepreneurial innovation and energy. But the Invisible Hand was repeatedly lifted at the elbow by the Government, which opened the way to new areas for economic activity and then replaced the Hand in a new position from which it could go on to perform its magic.

Brad DeLong

intervention (at least to establish property rights and ensure the rule of law). And hidden beneath the mathematics, the key assumptions that allow the First Fundamental Theorem to make any sense at all are the existence of property rights, and the idea that contracts can be written and enforced.

In addition to this, the same mathematics that 'proves' the theorem also shows why, in practice, the conditions necessary for it to hold are unlikely ever to be fully satisfied. Not only do the markets we normally think about (for buying and selling goods today) have to work, but so do futures and insurance markets. Moreover, everybody has to have the same knowledge and information, and there must be no monopolies and no 'externalities' such as pollution or congestion. Other even less realistic conditions, such as the absence of bankruptcy or limited liability, are also necessary, and any of these 'market failures' mean that the invisible hand can no longer be guaranteed, in Smith's words, to promote the interest of society as a whole.

Government intervention

So, the invisible hand provides arguments for both supporters and opponents of government intervention in markets. For some, it makes a case for limiting government intervention to the basic legal framework within which markets need to operate. Beyond that, there is little or no case for intervention. This interpretation of Smith's writings was invoked to oppose child labour laws in the 19th century and minimum wages in the 20th, as well as to argue for free trade and against protectionism. Well-meaning government intervention, it suggests, will just make things worse. For others it is the ways in which the market, and hence the invisible hand, can fail that matter most. Smith was particularly keen to point out that price signals, and hence the invisible hand, could not work if there were monopolies, established either by government fiat or by collusion. In his own words, 'People of the same trade seldom meet together, even for merriment and diversion, but the conversation ends in a conspiracy against the public, or in some contrivance to raise prices.'

A more recent concern is that of externalities – that is, economic impacts that are not captured in market prices. No invisible hand will, of itself, ensure that individual companies or consumers reduce carbon dioxide emissions enough to stave off the dangers of global warming, because there is no market price paid by those responsible. Only government intervention of some kind, through regulation or taxes, can put some sort of price on damaging emissions.

It is also important to remember that the invisible hand is a statement about a particular form of economic efficiency, not about morality. There is nothing in either Smith's original formulation or in modern economics to say that the allocation of resources resulting from the functioning of markets is either just or fair.

The condensed idea
Efficiency doesn't require planning

10 Creative destruction

How do capitalist economies grow and prosper? What makes companies more efficient or innovative, or workers more productive, and hence the economy as a whole bigger? This is a deceptively simple question, without a simple answer. And it turns out that one essential component of success is failure.

In standard neoclassical models of capital accumulation, not all income is consumed. Either firms make profits, or workers save some part of their wages, and hence it is reinvested. So long as enough is saved to replace depreciating capital and add more, the amount of capital grows over time, and so does the economy. Meanwhile, at the same time, productivity increases because of technological progress. This lets the economy produce more with the same amount of capital and labour.

On the surface that doesn't seem like a bad description of how economies work at an aggregate level. It suggests that economies that save and invest more will grow faster, and indeed they do. It also suggests that technological progress will lead to growth, which seems obvious. And it argues that more backward economies could grow faster by catching up technologically with more advanced ones, which again seems to work in practice. It also suggests that growth rates in advanced economies should be fairly stable, and outside recessions they are.

Beneath the surface

But this picture appears to miss two important aspects of how economies actually work. First, although overall growth may proceed at a relatively modest and stable pace – 2 or 3 per cent a year in advanced economies – that's not true of individual businesses. Every year lots of firms go bust, while some may grow very fast indeed, and others sit somewhere in between. Second, where does the productivity increase really come from? In fact, it arises through everything from very mundane improvements in the organization of firms to the commercial application of cutting-edge scientific breakthroughs to produce new goods and services. Technological progress isn't something that just happens in university laboratories with no connection with what's going on in the wider economy.

First Marx, and then in much more detail the Austrian economist Joseph Schumpeter, pointed out that simply looking at the steady accumulation of capital was not enough to explain the dynamism of capitalism. Capital is not just created, it can also be destroyed. And, crucially, this destruction is necessary for growth. The market does not just reward firms that make profits – it punishes those that don't. Firms that don't make profits will go out of business (and those that don't make enough profit may be taken over or broken up). The resources they use – most importantly their workers, but also sometimes their capital, if it can be reused – will be reallocated to more productive firms.

Moreover, Schumpeter argued, technological progress was not something that was unrelated to the growth and destruction of capital. Rather, new firms would develop new products or processes so that they could capture markets from existing firms, or create entirely new markets. Either way, existing firms would be destroyed, along with jobs and investment, but this destruction was necessary for the economy as a whole to grow:

'The opening up of new markets, foreign or domestic, and the organizational development from the craft shop and factory to such concerns as U.S. Steel illustrate the process of industrial mutation that incessantly revolutionizes the economic structure from within, incessantly destroying the old one, incessantly creating a new one. This process of Creative Destruction is the essential fact about capitalism. It is what capitalism consists in and what every capitalist concern has got to live in.'

Modern researchers have found that firm creation and destruction is indeed one of the major drivers of growth in advanced economies. Most productivity growth seems to come not from existing firms becoming more efficient, but from new firms entering markets and old firms exiting. Similarly, most job growth comes from the expansion of a few relatively new and fast-growing firms.

This process may be accelerating; the average lifespan of a company in the S&P 500 has shrunk from more than 60 years in the 1920s to only 15 years today. Much of the growth in the world economy in recent years has come from companies that were tiny, or non-existent, as recently as the 1980s, such as Apple, Amazon or Alibaba.

The upside of an economic downturn

More controversially, Marx and Schumpeter also argued not only that continuous creative destruction on the level of individual firms was necessary for growth in a capitalist economy, but that occasional episodes of much more widespread firm destruction were also necessary. In good times, it's too easy for firms to survive, and even grow, without necessarily increasing productivity or developing new products. Economic crises are necessary to cleanse the economy of sluggish and non-productive firms, and to free up resources for the next phase of capitalist development. In other words, recessions and worse are not a 'bug' in the capitalist system, as both neoclassical economists and Keynes would have argued, but rather a feature.

From this perspective, although recessions may lead to short-term pain for some workers and firms, they are necessary for continued growth over the longer term. This also means that even well-intentioned government intervention to moderate their impacts, through fiscal or monetary policy at the level of the whole economy, or through help to individual firms, will ultimately be counterproductive. Indeed, some researchers argue that this is one reason for the relatively slow recovery, and very low productivity growth of most advanced economies (especially in Europe) after the 2008–9 financial crisis. In contrast to previous recessions, not that many firms actually went bust during the post-crisis recession, partly because interest rates remained very low for a long time. Instead, many stagger on like zombies, locking up capital and labour in unproductive uses.

> A host of zombie and future zombie corporations now roam the real economy. Schumpeter's 'creative destruction' – the supposed heart of capitalistic progress – has been neutered. The old remains in place, and new investment is stifled.
> Bill Gross

The condensed idea
Failure is necessary for growth

11 Growth

This isn't an economics textbook, but to understand how economists think about capital accumulation, wages, technological progress and growth, a little algebra can help. And while the Solow model of growth should not be thought of as representing reality, it can help us to think about how an economy really works.

The Solow model is the simplest possible model of growth incorporating both capital and labour. It can be written simply as an equation linking these two factors alongside technology:

$$Y_t = A_t F(K_t, L_t)$$

In other words Y_t (the total output of the economy at time t) is a function of the total capital stock (K_t) and the total amount of labour (L_t) multiplied by A_t, which represents the state of technology. The model also assumes that there are constant returns to scale: that is, if you double the amount of both capital and labour (and technology doesn't change) then you double output. This seems perfectly reasonable – two workers using one machine each can produce twice as much as one worker with one machine.

The model then allows us to trace the connection between capital accumulation and growth. The output Y must be either consumed or saved: if the latter, then it is invested, and the capital stock increases over time. We can also assume that the existing capital stock depreciates or loses value over time, in which case some of the new investment is necessary just to replace the depreciated capital. It turns out this very simple model has some important implications:

• Diminishing returns to capital. For a given amount of labour, adding extra capital will have less and less impact on output.
• If there is a fixed rate of depreciation, then at some point the amount of capital added will only just make up for this. Without technological progress or labour force growth, the economy will converge to a steady state – no growth.
• Even if population and labour force grow, the economy will still converge to a steady state, where output grows but output is constant.

• Economies that start off in different positions, in particular with different levels of capital stock per head, will converge, as long as savings rates in the poorer countries are as high or higher as those in the richer ones. That is, the poorer countries' growth will 'catch-up'.
• The model allows us to do what is called 'growth accounting'; that is, explaining how much of the economic growth we see in different countries over different periods is explained by growth in the labour force, how much by increases in the capital stock, and how much by productivity growth.
• In the long run, the main driver of output per head is technological progress, or productivity.

With some additional assumptions – in particular, competitive markets – the model also tells us what to expect about wages and profits, or returns to capital. In particular, wages should rise as capital per worker increases, and the share of output that goes to wages should stay roughly constant as the economy grows.

The 'middle income trap'

The model predicts that poorer countries, if they save and invest, and adopt better and more productive technologies, will grow faster than richer ones, eventually catching up. And some countries, especially in East Asia, have gone a long way to catching up with the more advanced economies. However, after some initial catch-up, most haven't. This has led the World Bank to identify what it calls a 'middle income trap' – most of the countries that were defined as 'middle income' in 1960 are still in much the same place, relatively speaking.

What explains the middle income trap, and what can we do about it? Almost certainly it relates to the broader issues described here: what government does well and badly, and how the broader society functions. Given the proportion of humanity that is in countries that are either in the trap, or might be in future – most of Latin America, China and India – whether or not they can escape it, is one of the most important economic questions of the 21st century.

Convergence and rising wages

There is certainly evidence that developing countries that invest more (as long as that investment was not wasted), have seen some convergence: first Japan, and then other East Asian countries, had very high savings and investment rates, and saw rapid catch-up growth. And wages do generally rise (contradicting the Marxist view) as the capital stock per worker rises. Perhaps most surprisingly, the labour share did remain relatively constant for a long period, although in recent years it seems to have declined somewhat.

But perhaps the most important conclusion that can be drawn from the model is that of the limitations of neoclassical economics. The model says changes in capital stocks or savings rates may change growth rates in the short term, but in the long run the end point is pretty much the same. The same is true of other changes to economic policy – for example, removing trade barriers or lowering taxes. They may help, or hurt, but they won't boost growth in the long run. Only improvements in productivity through technological progress can do that, and the simple version of the model has absolutely nothing useful to say about how this might change or grow.

Productivity matters

This hole does not mean the model is useless. On the contrary, it has focused economists on trying to understand where productivity growth comes from. The most important leap here has been in understanding the importance of 'human capital' – the fact that some workers, thanks to education, aptitudes, skills and experience, are more productive than others. Once human capital is allowed for in the model, some other things are easier to explain. For example, if all workers were the same, then returns on capital should be higher in countries with lower capital stock per worker (poorer countries) and so if capital can move freely, investment should flow there. But, for the most part, this is not the case – indeed, the US runs a large current account deficit, meaning investment is flowing from other countries (especially China) to the US, but as long as US workers are more productive than Chinese workers, for the same amount of capital, this need not necessarily be a paradox.

> Productivity isn't everything, but in the long run it is almost everything.
> Paul Krugman

Other extensions to the model can allow for the importance of factors such as 'social capital', the institutional environment and legal framework, and so on. This in turn has influenced our attitude towards economic development – so while in the 1950s and 1960s there was a strong focus on encouraging countries to increase capital investment to boost growth, modern policy focuses more on education and skills (human capital) and institutions and governance. What matters most depends on time and place, but for most economies, most of the time, growth remains the key challenge.

Is there some action a government of India could take that would lead the Indian economy to grow like Indonesia's or Egypt's? If so, what exactly? If not, what is it about the 'nature of India' that makes it so? The consequences for human welfare involved in questions like these are simply staggering.

Robert E. Lucas, Jr

The condensed idea
How economies grow

12 **Entrepreneurs**

The role of the entrepreneur in a capitalist system is to take risks, with their own time and/or money, in order to convert a new idea or invention into a profitable business opportunity. Without entrepreneurs, an idea or an invention might never become a product.

Economic growth, and indeed human progress in general, ultimately comes from human ingenuity in the widest sense: scientific discoveries, new inventions or just better ways of doing things. This is true of almost everything that makes me more productive, from my shoes to my computer; and it is also true of almost everything that I consume, from television to wine. But an idea or invention, on its own, may have little or no impact on the economy. Somebody has to turn it into a product that can be developed, produced, marketed and sold. This is where entrepreneurs come in.

Sometimes entrepreneurs are also scientists. Thomas Edison invented both the first practical lightbulb and the phonograph (alongside many other things). But he also founded numerous companies to bring his inventions to the market, including the first investor-owned electricity company. Other scientists, however, have no desire to engage in business – such as Tim Berners-Lee, who invented, but never patented, the World Wide Web – or simply aren't very good at it – like László Biró, who invented the ballpoint pen but never made any money out of it, and eventually sold the patent to a Marcel Bich (or Bic), who made rather a lot of money out of it.

The heroic entrepreneur

We tend to romanticize the figure of the entrepreneur – starting with nothing, taking risks, perhaps failing at first, but eventually introducing a new, life-changing product to the world, and becoming extremely rich in the process. This is contrasted with the faceless, suited bureaucrats who run large companies. In the 19th century, it was the likes of Edison; in the modern age, it is Bill Gates or Steve Jobs. But the solitary, heroic entrepreneur is something of a myth. There are few Thomas Edisons, and Bill Gates's success was cemented by a partnership, at a key moment in the development of Microsoft, with the much larger IBM.

Entrepreneurship is usually very much more complicated than someone working alone at their laptop on the next Google or Facebook. New products or businesses are not created by a single person in a vacuum. They usually need finance from a bank or an investor; the availability of skilled employees in the relevant field; and often access to ideas from those working on similar products. There is a reason why start-up companies tend to cluster together, whether in Silicon Valley and Berlin for technology start-ups, or Hyderabad and Geneva for biotechnology.

Direct or indirect government support can also be key, either in funding basic research or in providing the legal and regulatory framework that allows it to be commercialized. Former Vice-President Al Gore did not 'create the Internet', as he is sometimes (mis-)quoted as claiming, but the 1991 High-Performance Computing and Communications Act that he sponsored did fund the National Center for Supercomputing Applications, where the first web browser was developed by a team including Netscape founder Marc Andreessen.

What is probably true, though, is that a relatively small number of entrepreneurial start-ups do have a disproportionate economic impact. While lots of people are self-employed, or start a small business, most are not developing new products. The most common occupation among the UK's 5 million-odd self-employed is that of taxi drivers, while most small businesses are shops, hairdressers and the like. These are valuable economic functions, of course, and many are 'entrepreneurial', but their overall economic impact is limited. By contrast, a few fast-growing firms make a big difference: OECD research shows that over half of all employment growth (and probably output growth too) is accounted for by such firms.

> Throughout the centuries there were men who took first steps, down new roads, armed with nothing but their own vision.
> Ayn Rand

Entrepreneurs – made, not born

Are some countries, or indeed people, more 'entrepreneurial' than others? It's uncertain whether President George W. Bush really did once complain to Tony Blair that 'the trouble with the French is that they don't have a word for entrepreneur', but it does reveal a common view in the US that Europeans, especially those from more social democratically inclined economies such as France, are somehow less likely to take risks. But in fact, the evidence to support this idea is far from clear. Perhaps having a stronger social safety net means that people will be more, not less, inclined to take risks, knowing that if they fail at least they won't fall into abject poverty? For example, Sweden, with one of the strongest welfare states in Europe, also does very well on most measures of entrepreneurship.

Similarly, various ethnic groups are often described as being very entrepreneurial, ranging from the Jews to the Gujaratis, and the Lebanese to the Hong Kong Chinese. In fact, it's quite difficult to find an immigrant group that hasn't been thus described at some point in its history, and this once again suggests that entrepreneurship isn't an individual or racial characteristic, but one that depends on the environment. Immigrants, often excluded by government and big business and lacking much in the way of capital or established business networks, have a strong incentive to try to make it on their own.

So we really shouldn't think about entrepreneurs as brilliant individual figures who succeeded through sheer force of will and strength of character, nor indeed as people who were just lucky enough to be in the right place at the right time (although both of these undoubtedly help). Instead, while they are one essential ingredient in a successful economy and society, they are also part of that economy and society, not separate from it. Government policy, from education to the welfare state, can either help or hinder, and entrepreneurs are made, not born.

The condensed idea
Linking inventions and products

13 Firms

I n all modern economies, the vast majority of private sector output is produced by firms – that is, companies, corporations, partnerships, or some other organization that exists primarily to make a profit. While lots of people, from shop owners to many doctors to farmers, are self-employed, they typically account for no more than one in five workers, and even less in terms of production. As economies develop, self-employment tends to shrink, and more and more people work in firms.

Why do firms exist? Capitalism necessarily involves individual motivation to make a profit, in contrast to an economy where other motivations or mechanisms are at work, like state control or altruism. But most economic activity in capitalist economies takes place within organizations that do not rely primarily on the profit motive to motivate individuals. Firms generally operate on the basis of 'command and control' – that is, there is a hierarchy, with someone at the top making the key decisions, and these being passed down the chain to those whose role it is to carry them out. Other mechanisms also operate: firms may be more or less consensual, with decisions being made by committee or consensus, and some allow workers a role in decision-making. The profit motive applies at the level of the firm as a whole, but not mostly for individuals, and it is individuals who take decisions and ultimately do the work.

So why are we not all self-employed? In principle, any economic activity could be conducted on the basis that all participants were self-employed, with a web of individual contracts and mechanisms for setting prices and sharing profits. But in practice that's impossible, even in a small firm. If I want you to deliver a presentation on marketing my new product at a meeting next week, how much should I pay you? What share of the profits on this new product should we get – after deducting payments to the people who actually make it and sell it? And so on. In a firm, we all get wages, and the profits go to the owners of the firm (which may be the original founders, shareholders, partners or sometimes even the workers, though even then the allocation of profits is generally separate from the payment of wages).

Reducing transactions costs

So organizing production in firms avoids the 'transaction costs' involved in having to set or negotiate prices for everything. And firms also share risk: as a worker, my success and my job depend not just on my own skill and luck but on that of the firm as a whole.

So if transactions costs are so bad, why don't we just have one big firm that produces everything? This was the thinking behind at least one strand of socialist economics: if all production was planned centrally, then surely just as much could be produced as under a decentralized system, without any transaction costs. But this doesn't work in practice – the price signals provided by some types of transaction are invaluable, both in giving firms information on what people actually want, and value, and in providing an incentive to improve and innovate.

And while central planning is not in fashion almost anywhere, largely private firms create their own problems. In a large company owned by shareholders, almost nobody – the chief executive, the board, the senior managers or the workers – has an incentive to make the firm as efficient and profitable as possible. The shareholders, who in theory do have most incentive, do not directly manage the company, and are often at several removes from it. And even when attempts are made to incentivize efficiency through contracts – pay and bonuses for senior management, for example – these can often do as much

> A lot of entrepreneurs hate big companies. But if you hate them so much, why are you trying to build a new one? The truth is, as soon as a start-up has any kind of success whatsoever, it will face big company problems.
> Eric Ries, US businessman

harm as good because such contracts inevitably also distort people's behaviour (transaction costs again!). In practice, then, decisions taken within firms are driven partly by the interests of the firm and the profit motive, but partly by individual self-interest, partly by the way committees and bureaucracies function, and partly by the idiosyncrasies of the firm's internal structures. It's not pretty, but it works, most of the time.

So firms, and economies where most production is carried out in firms, are inevitably a messy series of compromises and trade-offs

Uber

The taxi 'firm' Uber is a well-known example of the contemporary evolution of the firm, for good or ill. Uber claims not to be a firm in the conventional sense, but rather just an 'app'. Its drivers are not, legally, employees, but self-employed contractors who use Uber to find and connect with customers. The transaction costs that previously made it more efficient to organize taxi drivers in firms have been substantially reduced by new technology. This has its advantages (flexibility and freedom for the driverss, reduced risk to Uber), but also its downsides. Uber drivers have none of the security of regular employment and assume all the risk, while Uber's customers have few rights, since, legally, they aren't actually customers. Will more firms look like Uber? Probably. Will that solve the inherent tensions and contradictions described here? Probably not.

between the different potential downsides of different forms of organization. The result is different firm sizes and structures, driven not just by the market but by other economic and social forces. The textbook capitalist economy, like the textbook socialist one, doesn't, and can't, exist.

The gig economy and the death of the firm?

These trade-offs also change over time. In the 1950s and 1960s, large firms seemed to be the dominant form in the US and other advanced economies. In *The Organization Man*, William Whyte criticized the resulting conformity and lack of creativity, coining the term 'groupthink'. In recent years, however, there has been a rapid growth in small firms, start-ups and self-employment. This is often romanticized (we have all read stories about young people who start up tech companies and are millionaires in their 20s, and politicians love to talk about a 'nation of entrepreneurs') but it is by no means all rosy. The most common occupations for self-employed people in the UK are taxi driving and construction work, while some companies use 'self-employment' as a way of transferring risk to subcontractors who are no longer employees: the so-called 'gig' economy. This may work well for some, younger and more flexible workers, but for most people it is not attractive in the long term.

It's difficult to know what firms will look like in 20 or 30 years, but my forecast is that talk of the death of the firm and the growth of the gig economy will prove to be exaggerated. Both owners and workers will still want the stability guaranteed by a contractual, rather than one-off, relationship, and while some transaction costs will be reduced, others will increase. Firms have their downsides, but they will remain a key mechanism for dealing with the messiness of real-life markets.

> Many Americans are making extra money renting out a spare room, designing a website, even driving their own car. This on-demand or so called 'gig' economy is creating exciting opportunities and unleashing innovation, but it's also raising hard questions about workplace protections and what a good job will look like in the future.
> Hillary Clinton

The condensed idea
We can't all be self-employed

14 Banks

I t was in the rich trading cities of Renaissance Italy that something recognizably like modern banks emerged. And it was the goldsmiths of London, shortly thereafter, who began to issue notes in return for deposits, which they then lent on to borrowers in a forerunner to banks' modern role in money creation.

Most economists see modern banks as playing three main roles in the economy: as an intermediary between savings and investment; as a means of mediating between timeframes for savings and loans; and as a way of creating money itself.

Firms require investment to grow, and while some may be able to finance themselves – originally from the savings of their owners or founders and later from retained profits – most need to borrow at some point. Equally, other owners of capital (people who directly or indirectly own firms whose profits they do not want to reinvest, or workers who are earning more than they are consuming) want to be able to make a return. In theory, buyers and sellers of capital could simply negotiate loans bilaterally; in practice, banks centralize this. They pool savers' capital and assess the risk of potential loans.

Companies that borrow for investment want long-term loans so their investment has a better chance to make a return; but savers often want instant, or relatively quick, access to their savings. If loans were negotiated individually, this would be hard, but banks can pool short-term deposits and make long-term loans.

Finally, while banknotes and coins can generally only be issued by state-owned central banks (see Chapter 16), most money is created not by central banks, but by private ones. By making a loan, a bank doesn't just recycle money – it *creates* it, by allowing the borrower to withdraw cash or write a cheque. Borrowers want a loan so they can spend the money, and when they do, it finds its way back into the banking system, creating a new deposit corresponding to the original loan.

A risky business

All these functions are essential, but each creates risks – and taken together, even more so. By pooling, saving and lending, banks pool risk, protecting lenders against the danger of one borrower not being able to repay. If several borrowers can't repay at the same time, however, the bank itself may be in danger of failure, threatening all its savers. And this problem is made worse by borrowing short and lending long: if many savers want their money back at once, then even if the loans are perfectly good, the bank may not be able to pay them their money – it does not keep the cash sitting around, since that would defeat the whole purpose of the bank. This can easily become a self-fulfilling prophecy, known as a 'run on the bank': if I see that you are worried enough to withdraw your money, then maybe I should be doing so too.

So banks face both solvency risk (are the loans, as underlying assets, worth enough to pay back the deposits?) and liquidity risk (will too many savers want their money back at the same time?). These risks matter not just to the banks, and to individual savers and borrowers, but to the economy as a whole, since if a large bank fails it can send shockwaves through the whole economy.

For these reasons, banks get special treatment from the legal and regulatory system. Most importantly, they are subject to capital requirements; that is, they cannot simply borrow and lend out an extra $100, but also have to provide an extra $4.50 in assets that are not lent out (under the latest version of the international rules, known as Basle 3). So, very approximately, for every $100 loaned, the bank could 'lose' $4.50 on loans going bad before becoming in danger of insolvency. Furthermore, to prevent runs, most countries have at least some form of deposit insurance: small savers at least are guaranteed to receive their money back in the event of a bank failure, out of a fund collectively financed by the banks. In return, banks also get special privileges – in particular, a bank that is in trouble will often be given emergency loans by the central bank, and, in extreme cases, be 'bailed out' directly by government.

Are these trade-offs – extra regulation and extra help, sometimes including taxpayers' money – good value for the rest of us? It's very difficult to tell. But the contrasting experience of the Great Depression (when literally thousands of banks went bust in the US and across Western Europe) and the 2008–9 financial crisis (when most were rescued, bailed out or taken over) suggests they probably are. By preventing a complete collapse of the banking system, governments and regulators probably averted a much more serious depression that time round, although that does not make it any more palatable to see senior bankers escape the consequences of bad business decisions that in any other industry would have led to unemployment and bankruptcy.

Shadow banking

The traditional role of banks, increasingly subject to detailed regulation, has recently been challenged by new technology and financial innovation. All of the key functions outlined above can now, in principle, be performed by entities that aren't actually banks, but are instead part of what has become known as the shadow banking system. Peer-to-peer lenders use online exchanges to match savers directly with companies that need finance. Money market funds, which may be managed by banks but are not insured and are much less tightly regulated, offer the convenience of easy access to savings, while hedge funds pool capital from (generally wealthy) investors. Even the monopoly on money creation, perhaps the core function of the banking system, is being challenged by Bitcoin and no doubt others to come.

The future evolution of the banking system is impossible to predict – but its core functions are likely to remain necessary, and the inherent accompanying risks are unlikely to vanish. So banking, in one form or another, is likely to remain distinctive from other businesses, with both special privileges and special regulation.

I sincerely believe that banking establishments are more dangerous than standing armies, and that the principle of spending money to be paid by posterity, under the name of funding, is but swindling futurity on a large scale.
Thomas Jefferson

The condensed idea
With great power comes great responsibility

15 The role of government

For devotees of free-market capitalism, the role of the state is simply that of an impartial referee. As philosopher Robert Nozick put it, government intervention should be 'limited to the narrow functions of protection against force, theft, fraud, enforcement of contracts and so on'. But for the majority of economists, even those who accept a market-based framework, this does not go far enough.

In Nozick's extreme ideal, the state would simply provide a legal and judicial framework to define and enforce the property rights essential for a capitalist economy to function, with anything else seen as an infringement of liberty. Most economists, however, would argue that there are lots of other functions that the state can (either directly or indirectly) play an efficient role in providing. These are 'public goods' – services that all, or a large proportion of the population, benefit from, and that are difficult or impossible to directly charge for. Such services range from clean air and well-maintained roads to more disputed areas, such as basic education.

Although often presented as neutral, both of these positions are in fact anything but. The legitimacy of property rights, for example, depends very much on your perspective – on which rights are enforced, and how. At one point or another, most of the land in the United Kingdom and many other countries was acquired either by force, or by the coercive power of an absolute monarchy (see Chapter 2). It is therefore difficult to think of any coherent philosophical rationale that justifies the current patterns of ownership.

This point is not just historical, and does not just apply to land. Intellectual property rights, such as the duration of patents, what can and cannot be patented, and copyright law, are increasingly central to modern economies. Should companies be able to patent genes? How long should the inventor of a life-saving drug have the exclusive right to charge whatever price they want? There is no right answer to these questions – but it is the role of the state to find one.

Similarly, beyond the basic functions of national defence and law and order, the question of what constitutes a genuine public good is hotly disputed both among economists and more widely. Does it include education, which benefits both society as a whole but also individuals and families? What about the provision of healthcare and pensions? The answers to these questions are neither obvious, nor value-neutral, and they change over time.

Marx's view was more cynical. For him, the role of the state in capitalism was simply to do whatever was necessary in order to ensure that capitalism could continue to function in the interests (of course) of capitalists:

> 'The executive of the modern state is nothing but a committee for managing the common affairs of the whole bourgeoisie.'

Arguably, the 2008–9 financial crisis demonstrated the force of his position: when it came to the crunch, governments, almost regardless of their political colour, were quite prepared both to nationalize and bail out large banks, since the alternative was a wholesale collapse of the banking system, with incalculably damaging impacts on the capitalist system itself – not to mention the general population.

The changing role of government

In practice then, the role of the state in capitalist economies differs, both between countries and across time. Consider, for example, state involvement in the provision of healthcare. In most countries (with the notable exception of the US) the state guarantees healthcare to more or less the entire population, but there is a huge variety of different systems. In the UK, free healthcare is delivered by state-owned entities staffed mostly by state employees. In many other countries, most funding is from the state or

> I predict future happiness for Americans, if they can prevent the government from wasting the labours of the people under the pretence of taking care of them.
> Thomas Jefferson

through social insurance managed by the state, but services are often delivered by charities or the private sector. And even in the US, where the system is mostly private, insurance for the poor and the old is financed by taxation. What is clear, however, is that no government in an advanced economy can or should simply leave healthcare provision to the market.

Looking forward, there are very different visions of the state. Some continue to argue that technological change makes state provision less and less relevant. In particular, the case for public goods often relies on either information failures (in healthcare, for example, where consumers are rarely in a position to question the judgment of those who are providing services) or the lack of markets (for example, in pensions and other welfare benefits). But information is far cheaper and more widely available, and financial and other markets far more sophisticated, than they were at the invention of the welfare state. Many countries have sought to encourage much more private provision on pensions, for example.

> Better the occasional faults of a government that lives in a spirit of charity than the consistent omissions of a government frozen in the ice of its own indifference.
>
> Franklin Roosevelt

On the other hand, the increasing complexity and interdependence of modern technology means that the state's role in innovation, technological progress and regulation is far greater than it used to be. The origins of the underpinning technologies, from the Internet to the World Wide Web, can often be traced back to state agencies. As Italian-American economist Mariana Mazzucato points out, even a popular, profitable private sector product like the iPhone relied on state intervention at numerous points in its development.

Moreover, while the traditional welfare state has come under severe pressure in recent years, the basic imperative behind its creation (that if capitalism as an economic system is to be politically sustainable, the state needs to provide a measure of collective economic security) remains as strong as ever. And perhaps it has even grown stronger, as technological developments leave some workers increasingly insecure. The libertarian vision of a minimal state is as far away as ever – and for those who want capitalism to actually work in practice, not just in theory, that's probably a good thing.

The growth of the state

As economies grew more complex and prosperous, the role of the state expanded. Government expenditure as a share of the whole economy grew steadily, with occasional upward surges driven by wars. But this process seems to flatten off in the 1970s, since when there has been no clear trend. On the one hand, the health and education sectors, in which the state has a big role almost everywhere, are increasingly large shares of the economy, while an ageing population means that pensions are far more costly. On the other, technological progress means that some things that used to be obvious public goods are no longer so: postal and telecommunications services, for example, are now increasingly provided by the private sector.

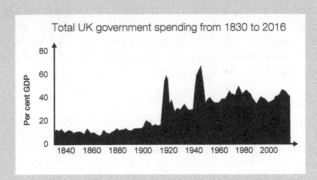

Total UK government spending from 1830 to 2016

The condensed idea
Government has an essential role in economic development

16 Central banks

Although they often started off as private institutions, central banks are completely different institutions to private ones, with very different functions. Rather than lending money to private enterprise, they control, either directly or indirectly, the creation of that money in the first place. And, by setting interest rates, they determine money's 'price'.

Central banks evolved as a way for governments to use their control over the issuance of currency in order to fund the state, and still play a key role in regulating the financial system. At the end of the 17th century, the Bank of England, the first modern central bank, was incorporated in order to lend money to the government to finance one of its many wars with France. In return, it was given authority to issue banknotes. Although initially private, over time it acquired other functions, and became essentially part of the state. With most countries on the gold standard in one form or another (see Chapter 6), the key function was to maintain the value of the currency and keep prices stable.

Mission creep

Yet it soon became clear that responsibility for managing the currency could not be separated from responsibility for the financial system as a whole. During the 19th century, there were periodic financial crises and bank runs. Walter Bagehot, an early editor of *The Economist*, formulated the principle that central banks could and should stabilize the system by lending to private banks during a panic – though only if the underlying solvency of the bank was assured. This in turn meant that the central bank had to be involved in regulating and supervising private banks. With governments mostly balancing their budgets, central banks became key to the management of the economy.

However, the Great Depression and the collapse of the gold standard represented a huge challenge to this approach. Indeed, it transpired that maintaining financial and broader economic stability was incompatible with the standard. Governments pressed for lower interest rates and devaluation, and countries that left the gold standard, as Britain did in 1931, recovered far more quickly than those, like France, which tried to maintain it as long as possible.

In the post-war era of Keynesian economics (see Chapter 28), central banks lost many of their responsibilities for economic management. Exchange rates were managed under the Bretton Woods system, while politicians used fiscal policy (tax and spending) to steer the economy, and incomes policies or price controls to restrain inflation (the general level of price rises across the economy). While this approach delivered stability and growth in the 1950s and 1960s, it came unstuck in the 1970s as inflation appeared to be spiralling out of control.

Milton Friedman and monetarism

It was Milton Friedman and his successors who provided the intellectual underpinning for the era of modern central banking. First, Friedman argued that central bankers, and in particular the Federal Reserve, bore a large share of responsibility for the Great Depression, since they had allowed the money supply (the quantity of money circulating within an economy) to collapse. Second, he argued that trying to manage demand through fiscal policy was a mistake – instead, macroeconomic management should aim at maintaining price stability, or at least low and stable inflation. This would best be achieved by using interest rates to ensure that the money supply

The Bretton Woods system

In July 1944, with war still raging, delegates from the allied nations met at Bretton Woods in New Hampshire, UK, to establish the framework for post-war international economic relations. Keynes represented the UK, while the US delegate, and key author of the plan that emerged, was Harry Dexter White. The 'Bretton Woods system' of fixed but adjustable exchange rates (ultimately underpinned by the convertibility of the US dollar into gold) was designed to avoid both the inflexibility of the pre-Depression gold standard and the instability that had followed its collapse. It did this largely successfully, providing one of the pillars of the rapid economic growth of the post-war years. However it disintegrated in the early 1970s as rising inflation at home and the Vietnam War abroad undermined US political and economic hegemony.

growth was slow and relatively stable. Friedman's dictum that 'inflation is always and everywhere a monetary phenomenon' set out the approach known as monetarism.

Central bankers take control

So in the 1970s and 1980s, control over macroeconomic management largely passed back from elected politicians to central banks. Income and price controls were gradually abandoned, fiscal policy was discredited as a way of managing demand, and monetary policy reassumed primacy. Sharp rises in interest rates, led by Paul Volcker as chair of the US Federal Reserve, eventually succeeded in reducing inflation. However, crude monetarism was abandoned fairly quickly, both in theory and in practice: it soon became apparent that targeting the money supply was not a very practical way of controlling inflation, since there are many different possible definitions of money, and as soon as one was adopted as a target, it seemed to stop working.

> In the 2000s, most central bankers failed to highlight — or even acknowledge — the risks building up in the banking system, Yet ironically, central banks emerged from the crisis more powerful than ever.
> *Financial Times*

Instead, 'new classical' and 'new Keynesian' economics focused more on the importance of expectations (what individuals and firms expected to happen to prices and wages) and the credibility of policymakers. This only made central bankers even more powerful: in order to ensure that they were credible in promising to keep inflation low, they had to be given independence from elected politicians. And the importance of 'expectations' means that it's not just what central bankers do, in terms of setting interest rates that matters – it's what they say as well.

Central bankers entered the financial crisis of 2008–9 with unchallenged dominance over macroeconomic policy. At the same time, however, their job appeared to be not particularly difficult – simply a matter of setting interest rates to achieve price stability. The crisis changed all of this. Not only did it put the use of fiscal policy back on the agenda, but, as interest rates fell to zero, central banks were forced to contemplate policies that would have been unthinkable in the era of stability – directly purchasing government debt (so-called

'quantitative easing') or even simply printing money and handing it
to the public ('helicopter money'). In 2012, Mario Draghi, president
of the European Central Bank, even had to save the euro currency,
and perhaps the entire European Union, by promising to do 'whatever
it takes' (it was never quite clear what he meant by this, but it
seemed to work).

Even years after the crisis, central banks face a dilemma. More than
ever, they are held responsible for ensuring economic stability and
averting crises (and, especially in the Eurozone, this raises questions
about democratic accountability). But with interest rates stuck near
zero, and other policies also apparently ineffective, they may no longer
have the tools to deliver. The image of the all-powerful central banker
is unlikely to survive another crisis.

The condensed idea
Central banks are powerful –
but they're not really banks

17 Trade unions

Are trade unions a fundamentally anti-capitalist, or anti-market, institution? Adam Smith set out what still remains the classical textbook view: 'The workmen desire to get as much, the masters to give as little, as possible. The former are disposed to combine in order to raise, the latter in order to lower, the wages of labour.'

Although in principle Smith disapproved of any interference with the market mechanism, he was fundamentally sympathetic to the workers. Writing in the latter half of the 18th century, he saw the combination of masters, or capitalists, to reduce wages as both much more common in his time, and far more damaging to society than any trade union. He was therefore more worried about profits being too high at the expense of workers than the opposite.

The workers' struggle

Not so the British government, which saw trade unions as the real threat (hardly surprising at a time when only the relatively prosperous could vote, and hence Parliament represented the interests of employers and landowners). The Combination Act of 1799 and its successors effectively prohibited unions, and was justified by reference to Smith's theories, but the real objective was to reduce the economic and political power of the new working class. This wasn't limited to industrial workers: the Tolpuddle Martyrs, who were tried, convicted and deported to Australia for joining a trade union, were agricultural labourers.

Nineteenth-century Britain saw a long struggle, waged in workplaces, on the streets and in Parliament, to secure the rights of workers to organize themselves. That same struggle was to be repeated in many other countries, sometimes peacefully and sometimes violently. By the end of the century, trade unions were more or less legal in most industrializing nations. But in many countries the trade union movement was split between those who saw their role as limited to securing improved wages and working conditions within the existing economic system, and those who saw this as merely a stepping stone towards more fundamental changes in the economic and political system that would ultimately put workers in charge.

Mostly, this conflict was resolved in favour of the former group. In post-war Europe and the US, unions (even if they retained some formal commitment to full-scale socialism) became an integral part of a mixed, but still essentially capitalist, system. In many countries they came to play a significant formal or informal role in economic governance, whether through their role in the health system in France, or on company boards in Germany. In the European Union and some of its constituent countries they are formally recognized, alongside employers' associations, as 'social partners'. And they play a key role in both financing and providing organizational support to social democratic parties in many countries.

Decline and fall

In the advanced economies, however, the economic and political power of unions peaked in the 1970s, after which it began to decline sharply. This was partly because of political overreach. For example, the 1978–79 'Winter of Discontent' in the UK, marked by widespread strikes from public sector unions, ultimately led to an election victory for Margaret Thatcher's Conservatives. Subsequent government measures to reduce union power culminated in the bitter defeat of the miners' strike in 1985. But despite such clashes with government, the decline of unions was mostly brought about by broader economic changes. The transition from a mostly industrial or manufacturing economy to a service-dominated one, with smaller workplaces, a larger female workforce, and greater diversity in the nature of people's jobs meant that fewer and fewer workers fitted the old-fashioned image of the trade unionist as a skilled male working on a production line. Unions were seen as primarily defending the interests of a shrinking number of workers in declining industries or the public sector, and painted as obstacles to economic progress. The proportion of workers belonging to a trade union has since fallen sharply in most countries, with fewer than 7 per cent of private sector workers in the US now belonging to a trade union, and their political and economic leverage has declined accordingly.

Modern challenges

So what is the future then for trade unions? Economic research suggests that the precipitate fall in union membership in most

Ironically, in countries where communist parties, supported by some trade unions, took political power, the role of unions generally became much diminished. After all, what role did unions have in reducing exploitation by the capitalist owners of the means of production once the state, or 'the people', were the owners? Trade unions in communist countries were generally treated as another arm of the ruling party, with the primary function of communicating the party's objectives to shop-floor workers. When workers wanted unions that would genuinely represent their interests, and tried to organize independent trade unions – such as Solidarity, founded in the Polish shipyards of Gdansk – they quickly came into political conflict with the communist state.

Such tensions are still apparent in China – a partly capitalist economy, but still a one-party state. Official trade unions have conflicting roles in representing workers' interests while maintaining close links to the government and communist party, while independent unions are at best tolerated and at worse repressed. This dynamic is unlikely to be sustainable indefinitely.

advanced countries over the last 40 years, and the sharp rise in inequality over the same period, are not a coincidence. Indeed, union membership remains high in many Scandinavian countries with greater social equality. And with inequality rising up the political agenda, this should be an opportunity: the very workers who are suffering most from globalization, the dominance of the financial sector, and the pressure on wages for unskilled workers are often the ones who in previous decades might have looked to unions to represent their interests.

But the fact that unions reduced inequality in the past doesn't mean they can in the future. In some countries, they have tried to expand their membership and reach beyond the traditional male working class to women, immigrant workers and low-paid employees in service sectors, but so far this has met with limited success. Meanwhile, the social democratic parties with strong financial and institutional links to unions are on the retreat in many countries.

The real challenge, it seems, is to make union membership relevant and useful to workers in growing sectors, and with changing patterns of work. What, for example, can unions offer to workers on temporary or zero-hours contracts, to the self-employed, or to those employed by multinational companies that can easily move tasks to cheaper locations? Does the future lie in trying to re-establish collective bargaining and collective action to improve pay and conditions, or in offering new types of services to different types of workers? The challenges of exploitation identified by Adam Smith have not gone away, but so far at least, trade unions don't appear to have the answers to their modern manifestations.

> The labour movement did not diminish the strength of the nation but enlarged it. By raising the living standards of millions, labour miraculously created a market for industry and lifted the whole nation to undreamed of levels of production. Those who attack labour forget these simple truths, but history remembers them.
> Martin Luther King

The condensed idea
Who will stick up for the workers?

18 Stock markets

Stock markets are markets for ownership and control of firms. They allow the original owners or founders to raise more money for new investment, so that the firm can expand and grow. But for better or worse, this also means giving up control over the management and direction of the company, as well as a share of the future profits.

The first stock markets emerged in Europe in the early modern era. Beurzen, or bourses were originally locations for trading commodities and debt, but they became places where shares in joint stock companies – those owned by shareholders, not just their original founders – could be bought and sold. The first stock trading took place in shares in the Dutch East India Company on the Amsterdam Exchange in 1602. Over the next two centuries, as the joint stock company model spread, so did stock markets.

Stock markets fulfil two key functions in a capitalist economy. They allow companies to raise capital for investment by issuing and selling shares to the general public, and they then allow the purchasers of those shares to resell them. This in turn means that investors are not locked in to a specific company for ever (which may make them more willing to invest in the first place), and it allows investors who did not buy shares in the company initially to do so later.

But over time the importance of the first function has declined. Most early stage companies now raise their initial investment capital from a mix of debt and private investors (private equity or venture capital) without issuing publicly traded shares. 'Going public' comes later, when the initial founders and investors want to sell part of the company for cash or use shares as a currency to buy other companies.

So if stock markets are not the main way companies raise capital nowadays, what is their economic function? In fact, these functions are now much more indirect. While markets do allow small investors (and those investing on their behalf, like pension providers) to purchase shares in firms, this usually involves buying from those who provided the original investment, rather than giving new capital to the firm directly. And because markets are public, with many buyers and sellers, they provide a transparent indication of supply and demand, and hence the market price for the shares at any one time.

The market for corporate control

Secondary trading in shares doesn't directly affect what the company itself does – after all, none of the money goes to the company for new investment. What does potentially affect the real economy, for better or worse, is the so-called 'market for corporate control'. If a company is performing well, its share price will rise; if not, it will fall. Such a fall may reflect events the company and its management can do nothing about, but it may also reflect management incompetence, or failure to take advantage of new opportunities. If so, there is money to be made: either another company, or a group of investors, can take advantage of the low price and buy enough shares to control the company, replace the management and adopt a more profitable strategy. The stock market therefore allows companies to take each other over or merge together, or enables activist investors to replace company management. In principle, this leads both to additional profits for investors and a more efficient economy in general.

But stock markets are not perfectly efficient (see Chapter 21) and hence neither is the market for corporate control. Share prices don't always fully reflect a company's long-term prospects, and some takeovers result not in improved performance, but in asset-stripping. Attacks on the short-termism of the stock market generally reflect a view that prices set by supply and demand in the market reflect only the short-term profit performance of the company. Fear of takeover could therefore lead to undue pressure on company management to maximize these profits, and this in turn could be at the expense of longer term investment plans that might be in the best interests of the company and indeed of the economy as a whole.

There may be some force to this criticism (and there are certainly examples of takeovers leading to poor outcomes for companies, their workers and customers). But arguably there are few things more fundamental to capitalism than this basic idea that the person willing to pay the most for something is the person who will make the best, or at least the most profitable, use of it.

Gambling at the speed of light

The past ten years have seen a huge increase in trading by computerized systems; on the main exchanges these are often responsible for the majority of transactions. Much of this trading is simply trying to take advantage of tiny price movements, and has no obvious underlying economic purpose – certainly it has nothing directly to do with the basic functions of stock markets described above and in the box on page 73. Defenders of 'high-frequency trading', and the computer algorithms that enable it, argue that the extra trading volume they produce increases liquidity (the ease and cost with which it is possible to trade), benefiting real investors like our German dentist or your pension fund, and hence ultimately making it easier for companies to raise capital. The evidence for this is, to say the least, mixed. But what is not in question is that the increased dominance of high-frequency trading over the last few years has resulted in an increase in stock-market instability. The 2010 'Flash Crash' (the result of an algorithm or algorithms going wrong,

> The Stock Exchange revalues many investments every day and the revaluations give a frequent opportunity to the individual (though not to the community as a whole) to revise his commitments. It is as though a farmer ... could decide to remove his capital from the farming business between 10 and 11 in the morning and reconsider whether he should return to it later in the week.
>
> John Maynard Keynes

deliberately or otherwise) wiped some 10 per cent off the US stock market. Other, similar, but smaller events followed. So far, none of these has done any significant permanent or systemic damage, but it is difficult to believe that the current system, in which more than half of all trading on some equity markets is carried out by algorithms, is sustainable indefinitely.

So what is the future for stock markets? Will computers take over completely, or will we find a way to return them to their original function of enabling companies to raise investment capital? At the moment, there is a risk that stock markets will become steadily less relevant to the real economy, and that cannot be good for capitalism.

> I don't know where the stock market is going, but I will say this, that if it continues higher, this will do more to stimulate the economy than anything we've been talking about today or anything anybody else was talking about.
> Alan Greenspan

The condensed idea
The market for control

19 The financial system

The financial system exists to channel capital from savers to productive investment. It does this via banks, which receive money from savers in the form of deposits and lend money to entrepreneurs and businesses, and via the stock market, where entrepreneurs raise money by selling shares.

But today's financial system is much, much more than just banks and stock markets. It includes insurance companies and pension funds, mortgage markets, and the whole of what is called the 'shadow banking' system, which loosely refers to any financial intermediary that channels money from lenders to borrowers but isn't a bank.

It's a big deal

Together, these various markets are big – far, far bigger than the underlying economic activities that they finance. For example, the original purpose of foreign exchange markets was to finance international trade, but daily turnover on these markets now exceeds $5 trillion, close to a hundred times the volume of the underlying trade in goods and services. Other markets are (on some measures) even bigger. Financial derivatives, for example, are securities whose value is dependent on the value of something else. They include futures and options, which are essentially bets on whether the price of something, like oil, will go up or down. Credit default swaps, meanwhile, provide insurance against a company or government not paying its debt. And interest rate swaps let banks or companies manage their exposure to future changes in interest rates (or take bets one way or the other).

The nature of derivatives means that they can be created almost without limit, so their value can far exceed the value of the underlying assets. In 2015, the notional value of outstanding derivatives contracts was more than half a quadrillion dollars, several times the annual world gross domestic product (GDP). And much of this trading, especially in stock markets and foreign exchange markets, is not carried out by humans, but by computer algorithms.

What explains this extraordinary growth in the size and scope of the financial system? And is it a natural development of capitalism, reflecting the importance of financial flows to productive investment, or a dangerous diversion that damages the real economy? Broadly, there are two views.

Just another market...

One opinion is that the creation and expansion of new financial markets, just like any other (legal) market, is a benign response to demand. Insurance markets allow people to provide against risk, while pension funds allow them to save for their retirement. Derivatives are mostly just another form of insurance: airlines can buy oil futures so that they don't suddenly find themselves bankrupt when oil prices go up, while banks can use interest rate swaps to hedge against future rate movements, which in turn allows them to offer fixed-rate mortgages to homeowners. All of this helps to ensure that money finds its way to the investments where returns are highest (which is good for both savers and businesses), and allows risk to be spread around the system to those who are best able to bear it. And while it is true that there are huge volumes of trading on some markets (much of it short-term and computer-generated) this too has a purpose. By providing liquidity (meaning that there are always buyers and sellers in the market), it reduces the costs to everyone and hence ultimately benefits consumers. In this view, there is no 'right' size for the financial sector – as with other sectors, it will be determined by supply and demand.

> When the capital development of a country becomes a by-product of the activities of a casino, the job is likely to be ill-done.
> John Maynard Keynes

Or parasitical on the real economy?

An alternative view is that finance, which should be the servant of the real economy, has become its master. In other words, when finance becomes an end in itself, and most people and institutions in the markets are trading to make money from trading, rather than to invest in productive activities, then the real economy will suffer. There is no reason to believe that the enormous volume of trading in the foreign exchange markets makes it any easier for firms to trade across borders, but it can lead to sudden, speculative swings in currencies, which are actively bad for such firms. Algorithmic trading in stock markets, meanwhile, may yield some very marginal increases in liquidity and reductions in trade costs, but it hardly encourages long-term investment. Meanwhile, salaries paid to those in the financial sector have exploded over the past 20 years, out of all proportion to the real economic value they create.

> In the financial system we have today with less risk concentrated in banks, the probability of systemic financial crises may be lower than in traditional bank-centred financial systems
>
> Timothy Geithner,
> (speaking in May 2006)

For those who support this latter view, the 2008–9 financial crisis was a vindication. Defaults on mortgage loans by some borrowers in the US (loans that had been packaged up and sold on as 'Collateralized Debt Obligations') led to a chain reaction of failures and a generalized loss of confidence in the system. It turned out that risk had not been shared, and still less allocated to those who were best equipped to manage it. Instead, it had been passed on to those who were too ignorant or foolish to know what they were buying. As a result, rather than making the system safer, this meant that relatively small problems could spread quickly.

Even for those who do not subscribe in full to this more negative view, the crisis showed that, in its current structure, the financial system needed reform – either through greater regulation to make banks hold more capital to guard against unexpected losses, by stopping firms selling exotic derivatives to people who didn't understand them, or by removing the implicit taxpayer subsidy of 'too big to fail' banks. But more than a decade on, perhaps the most remarkable thing is how little has changed. There is a lot more regulation (and many more jobs in both the financial sector and regulatory bodies as a consequence), but it is not clear what else has altered. Trading volumes have returned to their pre-crisis levels, as have bankers' salaries. Banks hold more capital, but the shadow banking system is as big as ever. Whether for political or economic reasons, fundamental reform seems beyond our grasp at present. In other words, don't bet against another crisis.

Just how complicated is the modern financial system?

At the height of the 2008–9 financial crisis, those of us working in the UK government had to quickly assess the state of the UK's large banks. These banks engaged in both retail banking (providing ordinary current and savings accounts, and making loans to homeowners and companies), investment banking and trading, and sometimes also wealth management. Naively, I thought their corporate structure would reflect this: a holding company, with subsidiaries for each of the main businesses. Instead, I discovered that one bank was in fact made up of several thousand different legal entities, most incorporated offshore in jurisdictions like the Cayman Islands or Jersey. Some were for individual transactions, while others were subsidiaries of subsidiaries. No doubt there was a more or less legitimate reason (often related to tax) for each one. But what struck me was how this made the job of anyone wanting to assess the 'riskiness' of the bank, be that a regulator or a senior executive, physically impossible. Almost a decade later, what has changed? Fortunately in this case, quite a lot: banks have indeed made radical changes to how they are structured. But does anyone – senior management, regulators or policy makers – really understand what's going on within them? I am not convinced.

The condensed idea
More than just a market

20 Limited liability

Most large companies are 'limited liability' companies; that is, if the company cannot pay its debts, then the owners and managers are not held personally liable for them, and can simply walk away. This corporate structure has its disadvantages, but it has also played a vital role in enabling capitalist economies to function.

The image of the heroic entrepreneur, willing to put his personal wealth and reputation on the line, is fundamental to our conception of capitalism. But we all know that, while many businesses start out owned and controlled by one person, a family or a few partners, the vast majority of large businesses are companies.

Companies limit personal risk

There are good reasons for this: the paradox is that while capitalism may be all about taking risks, one of the key inventions that made modern capitalism possible does so by limiting risk. Before companies existed, someone who wanted to go into business had to put their own personal wealth on the line. If things went wrong, they were personally responsible for any debts, and if they could not pay up, they went bankrupt. Not surprisingly, people were cautious about risky ventures – and banks were cautious about lending to them.

There was another downside as well: if a business required more capital than one person could provide or borrow, it was necessary to create a partnership. But partners were still personally liable for the debts of the business, so unless the partners both had confidence in each other, it was unlikely to work. This placed natural limits on how fast businesses could expand and how much they could grow.

Limited liability

The invention of the limited liability, or 'joint stock', company, solved these problems. The key breakthrough was the idea that a company could have a legal 'personality', separate from those of its owners, or shareholders. This allowed ownership rights (shares) to be bought and sold, potentially separating out the management of a company from its ownership, and hence making it easier to expand the capital base. It also made limited liability possible, meaning that the owners of the company were only liable for the company's debts up to the amount that they'd invested. So the company could go bankrupt without its owners also doing so.

The first economically important joint stock companies were those established to finance international trade in the early colonial era – enterprises that needed significant start-up capital and where the risks were very high. Perhaps the most famous of these was the East India Company, granted a royal charter (and trading monopoly) by Elizabeth 1 of England in 1600. In fact, the East India Company was something in between a company and a government-sponsored (but privately owned and managed) colonial venture. However the Dutch East India Company, established soon afterwards, was something much more akin to a modern company, with tradeable shares and limited liability.

> There was a time when corporations played a minor part in our business affairs, but now they play the chief part, and most men are the servants of corporations.
> Woodrow Wilson

These were still one-offs though. It was the Industrial Revolution, and the need for a way to secure finance for capital investment in factories, that established the joint stock company as the key legal form for businesses. In the UK, the Joint Stock Companies Acts of

A Shakespearean lesson

Shakespeare's *Merchant of Venice*, set in that city's heyday as the world's leading centre for international trade, provides a good illustration of the risks involved in trade at that time, and the downsides of unlimited liability. Antonio, the merchant of the title, is obliged to take out a loan from Shylock to finance his ventures. Although the financing terms are generous (in fact, the loan is interest free), the loan is 'secured' on Antonio's own flesh. If he had been incorporated as Venice Import & Export Limited, with shares sold to private investors, the subsequent unpleasantness might have been avoided.

1844 and 1856 allowed anyone to establish such a company, and provided for limited liability. Most countries have since introduced similar provisions.

Today, the vast majority of private sector business activity is conducted by limited companies, although that does not necessarily mean that their shares are publicly traded. Of course many people are simply self-employed, but the advantages of limited liability mean that, as soon as a business begins to grow, its owners generally seek to incorporate it as a company. Very few businesses employing more than a few people have unlimited liability.

Downsides and alternatives

However, there are downsides as well, both to the form companies take and to limited liability itself. In particular, owning shares in businesses that don't have much in the way of tangible assets may be quite risky. The main assets of many firms that provide business services such as law and accountancy are the knowledge, experience and client base of the people who work there. So while you could have shares in that firm, they're only worth anything as long as the employees stay around – and it's very difficult to tie them down to a company. For that reason, most such firms are still organized as partnerships rather than companies, so that key individuals still have their own capital invested in the business, and can't easily sell it on. It has been suggested that as physical capital (such as machines and other fixed assets) becomes less important, and the skill and knowledge of workers more so, partnerships will again become an increasingly common mode of ownership.

Another issue is that, while the very purpose of limited liability is to encourage risk-taking, you can have too much of a good thing – especially in the financial sector. In the run-up to the 2008–9 financial crisis, some banks were making very large bets, and as long as those bets went reasonably, shareholders (and well-paid bank employees) did very well indeed. When things went horribly wrong, limited liability meant that shareholders only lost what they had invested, although in some cases the losses were far larger. Instead, it was the people the failed banks had borrowed money from (and in too many cases, also governments and taxpayers), who ended up paying the bills. As a result, some have argued that in future many financial sector firms – especially those that engage in risky trading activities of one sort or another – should look less like joint-stock companies, and more like partnerships in which the key, highly paid employees are part-owners, and liable for the risks that they take.

The condensed idea
By limiting risk, companies allow risk-taking

21 Efficient markets

The Efficient Markets Hypothesis (EMH) states that asset prices fully reflect all available information, and that they adjust quickly to the arrival of new information. The implications of this are profound: the hypothesis suggests that it's impossible to find systematic patterns in market fluctuations, and therefore that 'technical analysis' of stock prices has about as much scientific basis as astrology.

The EMH builds on the Austrian economist Friedrich Hayek's view that one of the functions of markets is to aggregate dispersed information. In particular, he argued, participants in financial markets trade on the basis of their information and beliefs. This will in turn determine market prices, which thus will reflect all the information that is available to market participants.

You can't beat the market

Carried to its logical conclusion, the EMH means that stocks will follow what statisticians call a 'random walk' of price variations. Thus, there should be no way for investors to systematically beat the market, and there can be no such thing as a stock market bubble. And there's no point in trying to figure out where best to invest your money to make the highest return, or paying someone to actively manage your investments; an entirely random approach would do just as well. Some have even blamed the EMH for the financial crisis: former Federal Reserve Chairman Paul Volcker said 'it is clear that among the causes of the recent financial crisis was an unjustified faith in rational expectations [and] market efficiencies.'

But it's also important to be clear on what the EMH *doesn't* say. It doesn't imply that financial markets are always 'right', just that it's not possible to systematically or consistently predict what they are going to do. It does not say that some investment strategies won't yield higher returns than others, only that higher returns will come at higher risk. And it doesn't say (except in the 'strong' form of EMH, which even enthusiasts don't subscribe to) that you can't make money if you have access to some information (legally or illegally!) that nobody else knows about. It merely argues that once you start to use that information to trade, prices will adjust quickly and automatically.

There is now a substantial body of evidence that suggests investors would do well to pay attention to the EMH. Technical analysis (the use of past patterns and price trends to predict future movements) appears to be almost entirely useless. And it seems to be vanishingly rare for active managers to outperform the market consistently. The theory, encapsulated by economist Burton Malkiel, that 'a blindfolded monkey throwing darts at a newspaper's financial pages could select a portfolio that would do just as well as one carefully selected by experts' appears to be broadly accurate. In this respect, the EMH has been extremely influential: it certainly accounts for the increasing popularity of low-cost index funds, which track the market rather than try to beat it.

> I'm convinced that there is much inefficiency in the market. When the price of a stock can be influenced by a 'herd' on Wall Street ... it is hard to argue that the market always prices rationally.
> Warren Buffett

A paradox

But on the other hand, the spread of index funds illustrates the paradox at the heart of the EMH. If every investor believed it, then markets would stop being efficient, because no one would bother to seek out new information, or trade on it. If we all invested solely in index funds then the index would cease to have any meaning.

The EMH therefore depends on the existence of at least some investors who, in contradiction of the hypothesis itself, seek to outperform the market.

This is illustrated by a number of market 'anomalies'. For example, calendar year effects include the old adage 'sell in May and go away', and the January effect (a general rally in prices at the start of the year). The so-called small company effect, meanwhile, suggests that smaller companies appear to outperform the market, even accounting for risk. These may be real, but usually once they are identified, some investors will try to use them to make money – and the effects will largely disappear. So for practical purposes, this is a vindication of the EMH rather than contrary evidence.

> The hypothesis does not claim that the market price is always right. On the contrary, it implies that the prices in the market are mostly wrong, but at any given moment it is not at all easy to say whether they are too high or too low. The fact that the best and brightest on Wall Street made so many mistakes shows how hard it is to beat the market.
> Jeremy Siegel,
> *Wall Street Journal*

But a much larger challenge to the EMH is that posed by Robert Shiller, who argues that human psychology means that markets can be not only wrong, but consistently and predictably wrong. Shiller argued that this was the cause of 'bubbles' – episodes in which market prices systematically deviate from those implied by publicly available information, contrary to the EMH. Famously, in 2005 he predicted that the US housing market was in a bubble, with a crash as the likely outcome. He has also argued that stock market price–earnings ratios tend to revert to a long run average – in other words, investors could make money by buying stocks when prices are 'low' (relative to earnings) and selling when they are high.

Is it possible to reconcile these different views, as the Nobel Committee apparently did (see page 85)? Oddly enough, most economists manage it, arguing that most of us would be better off not trying to beat the market at an individual level, but at the same time believing that markets can be far from rational, and bubbles and crashes can do very real economic damage.

The EMH and the crisis

Did the Efficient Market Hypothesis really cause the 2008–9 financial crisis? At one level, of course not; it was caused by individuals and firms who took excessive risks and gambled with other people's money, and by governments who failed to regulate the financial sector properly. Some of this behaviour was greedy, and some of it was stupid, but none of it shows that either individuals or markets were behaving particularly irrationally, or that it was belief in the EMH that drove such behaviour. However there is no doubt that an unrealistically naïve view of the self-correcting nature of markets, and a view that they could not collectively be 'wrong', did contribute to these errors, both by market participants and governments.

The condensed idea
You can't beat the market

22 Financial crises

'**N**o more boom and bust', proclaimed the UK Chancellor of the Exchequer Gordon Brown in 1997. And indeed, by 2007, in common with many other countries, the UK had experienced some 15 years of more or less continuous economic growth. But by the end of 2008 the world had entered the worst economic and financial crisis since the Great Depression.

Mr Brown – by then prime minister – now found himself presiding over an economy that shrank by more than 4 per cent in just three months, and where a complete financial collapse was only averted by the effective nationalization of large parts of the UK's banking system. But to be fair to him, he was just making a catchy phrase out of what economists called the 'Great Moderation'. Everyone believed we had learned from the mistakes of the Great Depression; active macroeconomic policy management, combined with sensible regulation of the financial system, could prevent a financial crisis turning into a wider economic downturn. And we had also learned from the breakdown of the Bretton Woods system of fixed exchange rates (see Chapter 16) and the failures of simplistic Keynesian attempts to manage the economy with fiscal policy (that is, by varying the level of tax and public spending). Instead, monetary policy, directed by an independent central bank, could smooth out the business cycle and avert sustained rises in either unemployment or inflation.

And what about the financial system? Well, that could largely take care of itself. Although some regulation was required, financial innovations ranging from credit default swaps to mortgage-backed securities only made the system safer. By packaging and repackaging risk and selling it on, individual risks would be less concentrated, and those who could best manage it would bear the burden of any losses. Any problems with individual financial institutions could be easily contained. Or so we thought. The 2008–9 financial crisis, and the ensuing 'Great Recession', have led to a widespread rethink, particularly of whether the financial system as a whole is structurally unstable. American economist Hyman Minsky's (1919–96) 'financial instability hypothesis', put forward in 1992, could have been formulated to describe the Great Moderation:

'Stability leads to instability. The more stable things become and the longer they are stable, the more unstable they will become when the crisis hits.'

Minsky's argument was simple: a stable and successful economy encourages debt because, as long as things are going well, it will pay to take on debt. Investors who have greater 'leverage' (that is, a greater proportion of debt rather than equity investment) will see higher returns, because the equity holder gets to keep all of the profits, while debt only gets a fixed return. So as a stable economic situation develops, there will be more and more debt relative to a fairly fixed quantity of equity. Financial innovations will increase this still further, and central banks will be unable to keep up. The economy will grow, but debt and asset prices (stocks, housing, art, wine and indeed anything the wealthy like to 'invest' in) will grow even faster.

But eventually the music stops; some investment project, or set of projects, will go wrong. If the project has been financed largely by equity, this would have little in the way of wider economic consequences – just as the collapse of the first tech bubble in the early 2000s had little impact on growth or employment. But if the project is debt financed – as was the case with subprime mortgages in the US – then the consequences will ripple through the system. Other debtholders will want to reduce their exposures, asset prices will fall, and some markets may collapse completely. Even good businesses and sound investments end up being affected.

What we know about the global financial crisis is that we don't know very much.
Paul Samuelson

This proved to be an excellent description of what happened in 2008–9. Default, or just the threat of default, on a relatively small number of bonds led to a loss of confidence first in the financial institutions that were thought to be heavily exposed, and then in the wider system as a whole. This in turn led to financial markets seizing up entirely, bank failures and a collapse in world trade. Governments had learned the lessons of the Depression, and so swift action – bank bailouts, interest rates cuts, fiscal stimulus and finally 'quantitative easing' (where the central bank seeks to inject money directly into the economy) – prevented things from being nearly as bad as then. But it still couldn't prevent both a very sharp recession and a very slow (in much of southern Europe, non-existent) recovery. In the aftermath, output and wages in even the US and UK were left more than 10 per cent lower than would have been forecast in 2007.

Are crises inevitable?

So does this mean that financial crises and their economic consequences are just part of the natural (capitalist) order of things? Understandably, politicians and economists prefer to think otherwise, though no one believes any longer that the financial sector can be left to itself, with only 'light-touch' regulation. A raft of new rules has been introduced, designed in particular to restrict leverage and ensure that a failure of one or two financial institutions does not lead to panic and hence to a widespread or systemic failure. Many, however, think that this doesn't go nearly far enough, and would prefer a more wholesale approach to reining in the financial system. Keynes, who thought that although finance was necessary, its role in capitalism should be rather strictly limited, would probably have agreed.

> Speculators may do no harm as bubbles on a steady stream of enterprise. But the position is serious when enterprise becomes the bubble on a whirlpool of speculation. When the capital development of a country becomes a by-product of the activities of a casino, the job is likely to be ill-done.
>
> John Maynard Keynes

But Minsky would have been cautious about either thinking that the changes we've made so far will be enough, or that even more are needed. His hypothesis essentially says that the better governments and regulators manage the system (and the more stable they make it) the more they will breed overconfidence, and the worse the eventual crash will be when it comes. If that's the case, then financial capitalism, plus human nature, mean that occasional crises are inevitable, and we'd perhaps be better occupied in making sure that we have better contingency plans next time round.

The South Sea Bubble

'A company for carrying out an undertaking of great advantage, but nobody to know what it is.' This was, infamously, a genuine description of one of the many joint stock companies to go public in Great Britain in 1720 as part of what is still history's most famous stock market bubble. The South Sea Company had been founded in 1711, with a monopoly to trade between the burgeoning British colonies and South America. Unfortunately, since South America was part of the Spanish Empire, there was no realistic prospect of it ever actually making any money. So instead, the Company competed with the Bank of England to trade in UK government debt, which it did through a mix of bribes, swindles and what were effectively pyramid schemes. As its stock price soared, enthusiasm for investing in stocks grew, and many other equally dubious companies sprung up. The inevitable collapse in 1720 ruined many, and led to the imprisonment of the then Chancellor of the Exchequer. We may laugh now at the gullibility of investors and the venality of early 18th-century politicians but, as anyone who has studied the US subprime mortgage crisis of 2006–08 will know, human nature has not changed so very much.

The condensed idea
It will happen again

23 Debt

Debt, like money, predates capitalism, dating back to at least Mesopotamian times. But debt plays a particularly important role in capitalism because it is the main way that investment, either by companies or individuals, is financed. Indeed, debt is now more central to the modern financial system than stock markets.

At any given time, some of us want to spend more than we earn, while others are earning more than we spend. So our savings are mostly held in banks and pension funds, and these are lent to companies to invest, to individuals to buy houses, and to governments in order to finance that part of their spending that they do not cover by raising taxes.

Too much debt?

But can we have too much of a good thing? 'The world is drowning in debt', according to investment bank Goldman Sachs. This is more than a little ironic: it was Goldmans that helped Greece conceal just how much debt it was really running up in the 2000s, making the eventual crisis worse, but netting hundreds of millions of dollars in fees in the process. But apparently many countries – not just Greece, but also more economically sound ones like Japan – are sinking under too much debt. For instance in 2015 the International Monetary Fund warned that without action to control spending, Japan's debt will be three times the size of its economy by 2030.

Statements such as this are common, but they often include two common errors made when talking about debt. The first and most important of these is to ignore the fact that debt is, by definition, also an asset. A debt is a financial obligation owed by someone, or something, to someone else. In the case of Japan (and indeed many other indebted governments, such as Italy), the assets in question – the government debt – belong mostly to its own citizens and companies. 'Japan' isn't really in debt at all; rather, Japanese citizens have very large assets, many of them held in the form of debt issued by their own government.

The second error is to mix up a 'stock' with a 'flow'. Japanese government debt is equal in value to something more than twice the annual economic output of Japan. That sounds like a lot; but so what? A year is just an arbitrary time period. It would be just as accurate to say that it is equal to more than a hundred times weekly output, which makes it sound far worse – or less than 3 per cent of output every century, which is a lot less worrying. None of these comparisons is very useful in themselves, because it is meaningless to compare a total at one point in time with an annual figure like this.

It's who owes what that matters

So it is not so much the amount of debt that matters but its distribution – who owes what to whom. The 2008–9 global financial crisis was indeed a debt crisis, not a stock market crisis. At a global level, high savings in China and some other countries, such as Germany, kept interest rates down and meant that companies and households in other countries took on more debt than they could handle. The trigger for the crisis was the collapse of the subprime mortgage market in the US, where low-income households had been encouraged to borrow more than they were ever realistically likely to repay. It didn't stop there, and the crisis

> Annual income twenty pounds, annual expenditure nineteen pounds nineteen shillings and six pence, result happiness. Annual income twenty pounds, annual expenditure twenty pounds ought and six, result misery.
> Charles Dickens, *David Copperfield*

spread to Europe, particularly affecting countries where either governments (as in Greece) or, more commonly, the private sector (as in Ireland or Spain) had borrowed too much.

Was this just a glitch, or does it reflect something more fundamental about the destabilizing influence of debt? In particular, was it related to rising income inequality, particularly in the US? Capitalism needs consumers to generate demand and hence growth, but with the rich (who tend to save more) taking a larger share of the pie, the only way consumption could continue to grow was for the less well off to borrow money they hadn't earned and were never likely to repay. The worry is that unless we do something about the underlying problem of inequality, we will find ourselves in the same position again: in order to generate growth, ever-rising debt will be required, and eventually this will prove unsustainable.

Government debt

So what about the debt owed by governments? Contrary to some claims, there really is no evidence to suggest that the financial crisis was caused or worsened by high levels of government debt, except in the case of Greece. But the crisis – and then the pandemic – did leave governments with much higher levels of debt and deficit than before, and these debts will take years, maybe decades, to reduce. However, that need not be a problem in the short term: with interest rates still at very low levels by historical standards, even after recent rises, advanced economies such as the US, Japan and larger European countries have no immediate problem in financing their debts.

But it is perhaps precisely this – that governments find it very easy to borrow – that is particularly worrying for the future of the debt-based capitalist model. The fact that, even with high inflation, governments can borrow cheaply, is a signal that companies and households don't want to take on more debt. That could be because they think they've got too much already, and want to reduce rather than increase it (the 'debt overhang' hypothesis). If this is true, then until the overhang has been dealt with, investment and hence growth may remain low. It could be they don't think there are any attractive investment opportunities worth taking on debt for (a version of the 'secular stagnation' hypothesis – see Chapter 45). Or it could be a combination of both. Either way, it suggests that the prospects for future growth are poor – which is bad news at a time when the global

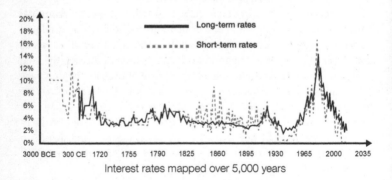

Interest rates mapped over 5,000 years

economy should be recovering strongly in the aftermath of the crisis and subsequent recession.

What can governments and central banks do? Well, they have kept official interest rates very low, and introduced extraordinary measures like quantitative easing (where central banks directly purchase government debt from the private sector) in order to encourage more lending and more debt. But so far it hasn't worked, and it might even be counterproductive if it just stores up future instability. Governments could borrow still more themselves, taking advantage of low interest rates to increase much-needed public investment, as well as boosting demand. Most economists think this makes obvious sense, but paradoxically, public and political fear of increasing public debt has so far largely blocked this route. More radical alternatives like a jubilee (systematic writing-off of debt) to reduce the debt overhang have also been suggested. But at the moment, the world still seems to be stuck, with both too much debt looking backwards, and yet too little looking forwards.

> If you owe your bank a hundred pounds, you have a problem. But if you owe a million, it has.
>
> John Maynard Keynes

The condensed idea
Can't live with it, can't live without it

24 Democracy

s capitalism conducive to democracy, or do the two conflict? The historical evidence seems reasonably clear. Although the development of capitalism and the spread of democracy don't parallel each other precisely, they do seem to run alongside each other.

For economic development to be sustainable, some protection of property rights is required, and that in turn requires the rule of law. If the ruler or the aristocracy can simply expropriate your property at will, there is little incentive to create wealth. But this doesn't in itself require democracy: as long as most people lived in rural areas and worked in agriculture for subsistence wages, there was no economic need to give them any direct say in how they were governed.

Capitalism upset the balance of power

This changed with capitalism. As the emerging middle class of businessmen, factory owners and those associated with them became economically dominant, they claimed their share of political power at the expense of agricultural interests. Early capitalist 'democracy', with its highly restricted franchise (generally of men with a reasonable amount of property) therefore prioritized, by design, the interests of the emerging capitalist class.

But this situation was inherently unstable. The growing industrial working class had its own interests and demands, both economic and political, that were expressed first mostly in trade unions (see Chapter 17) and then in political parties. Universal suffrage was the key demand of the Chartists in early 19th-century Britain, and while they were suppressed by force, history was largely on their side. Essentially the ruling class, Marx's emerging 'bourgeoisie', were faced with a choice: share political power (and hence accept some degree of economic redistribution) or resort to increased forcible repression, with the likely negative economic consequences that would bring.

So in the 19th century, in most but not all countries that saw a transition from an agrarian to an industrial capitalist economy, this was accompanied by successive expansions of the franchise. This process played out differently in different countries: in the UK it was largely peaceful and gradual, while in the US, the existence and then legacy of slavery meant that racial conflict influenced the development of democracy alongside class. In Western Europe, although many countries developed some form of democratic institutions as they industrialized, the process was far from even.

The first half of the 20th century saw two world wars, a Great Depression and consequent economic and political turmoil almost everywhere. But when the dust settled, virtually all advanced capitalist economies (primarily in Western Europe and North America) were democracies. The incorporation of female workers into the market economy, as women moved from mostly working on farms or at home into offices and factories, went alongside their right to vote.

The advance of democracy

Democracy and capitalism advanced further in the second half of the 20th century. Spain and Portugal, the remaining dictatorships of Western Europe, became democratic in the 1970s, and then in 1989 the fall of the Berlin Wall was followed by a surprisingly quick (although far from painless) economic and political transition in Eastern Europe.

At the beginning of the 21st century then, not all capitalist economies are democracies; and there are plenty of democracies where capitalism is relatively undeveloped. But nevertheless, the connection appears to be relatively strong. The few remaining countries that are aggressively anti-capitalist as a matter of policy (like North Korea) are also aggressively anti-democratic. Many other non-democracies are states in which most wealth derives directly or indirectly from natural resources (as in the Gulf States). As a result, there is neither a strong and economically independent bourgeoisie to demand and enforce property rights, nor an industrial working class that seeks political power and economic security.

History suggests that capitalism is a necessary condition for political freedom. Clearly it is not a sufficient condition.
Milton Friedman

So if capitalism and democracy go together, will most countries inevitably move closer to both? In the years after the fall of the Berlin Wall, this seemed to go without saying. But there are two obvious challenges to this view, centring on the world's two largest economies.

The Chinese paradox

First is China. China's model of capitalism differs considerably from that current in most countries, but it is by any measure the most successful example of capitalist development of recent times, and perhaps ever. China has seen as much economic growth in the last three decades as Britain did in the 19th century, driven by a similar migration of the rural population to urban centres to work in factories (albeit on a far larger and faster scale). But China has not seen parallel political development. 'Socialism with Chinese characteristics' could equally be described as capitalism with Chinese characteristics; what is certain is that China has, so far, taken its own path (see Chapter 35).

The second issue is that of rising inequality within rich capitalist countries. What Marx and others identified as an inevitable tendency for market processes to concentrate wealth among the owners of capital seemed to be contradicted by the post-war experience, as trade unions moderated wage inequality and democracy led to the establishment of welfare states, to a greater or lesser extent, in virtually all advanced capitalist countries. But recently income and wealth inequalities have widened again, particularly in the United States, the most technologically advanced country of all. Many would argue that this in turn has consequences for democracy, with the rich, and especially the super-rich, wielding a disproportionate degree of influence on the political process. At what point does this call democracy itself into question?

The condensed idea
People power versus the power of money

25 Conservatism and liberalism

I n contemporary political discourse, 'conservative' is often taken as a synonym for pro-market or pro-capitalist, while in the US, 'liberal' means someone who favours a larger role for the state and higher taxes. This usage has been common since the era of Ronald Reagan and Margaret Thatcher, who were both conservative icons and were proudly pro-capitalist. Historically, however, the meanings of these two terms were very different.

The classical liberalism of Adam Smith and John Stuart Mill, particularly in the United Kingdom, emphasized a particular view of freedom – both the freedom of a people to choose its own government and make its own laws, and the freedom to engage in economic activities without government interference. Edmund Burke, the founder of modern conservativism, accepted Smith's views of economics and favoured free trade and free markets, but he emphasized the importance of tradition and order in politics, society and the economy. In particular, he rejected the idea implicit in classical liberalism, that both economy and society would naturally tend towards the best possible outcome with a minimum of government interference.

But Burke did not reject change – instead, he argued that it was necessary to preserve the fundamental values of society:

'A state without the means of some change is without the means of its conservation.'

At first in the United Kingdom, and later elsewhere in Europe, the 19th century saw a struggle between conservatives attempting to preserve an old social and political order dominated by the aristocracy and landowning classes, and liberals representing the interests of the new capitalist class.

The philosophies of both sides, while both consistent with the development of capitalism in an economic sense, each contained their own internal political contradictions. The repeal of the Corn Laws, a series of price controls that had protected British agricultural interests from foreign competition at the expense of urban workers and hence of industry, split the Conservative Party. Later, the Liberals did not know how to respond to demands from the industrial working class, first for protection against exploitation at work (which necessarily required interference with the free market) and later for political representation and power. Over time, the free market capitalism advocated by both Smith and Mill disrupted English life and traditions in ways that would have horrified Burke.

The conflict continues

Notionally conservative, pro-capitalist parties have dominated politics in advanced industrialized countries since the rise of Thatcher and Reagan. In general, such parties support broadly market-based approaches to economic policy, less government regulation, and lower taxes and social benefits, all consistent with an approach to economic management that is designed to facilitate the smooth operation of the capitalist system.

Yet, particularly in an era of rapid globalization, capitalism is a dynamic force that tends to disrupt rather than perpetuate the existing social order. So the same period has also been an era of rapid social change, often driven by capitalism and opposed by the same political parties. For example, conservative parties facilitated the economic changes that led to the decline of the largely male industrialized working class, while at the same time decrying the rise in single parenthood and decline of the 'traditional' family – a social structure whose existence had been supported by the industrial model their own economic changes undermined. Globalization, and the breaking-down of all sorts of regulatory and technological barriers to international trade and exchange, has unsurprisingly led to a sharp rise in immigration flows as labour, too, responds to market forces. Yet such movements inevitably have significant social and cultural impacts that are often anathema to conservatives.

> But what is liberty without wisdom, and without virtue? It is the greatest of all possible evils; for it is folly, vice and madness, without tuition or restraint.
> Edmund Burke

These tensions are particularly visible in the United States, where conservatism implies visceral opposition to restrictions on 'economic freedom' through tax and regulation, but also support for government restrictions on individual freedoms such as the right to an abortion, to marry or to move to the US. In Europea, similar internal tensions are often manifested in opposition to the European Union – both for its supposed over-regulation and over-interference, but also for its efforts to liberalize trade and migration flows.

The 'third way'

Classical liberalism, meanwhile, is largely dead as a political movement; the constituency for those who both support a purist free-market approach to economics and a libertarian approach to social issues is small. Its nearest heirs were probably the 'Third Way' social democrats represented by Bill Clinton and Tony Blair. Like the classical liberals, they were consistent on economic and social issues. They welcomed globalization and accepted the deregulation and privatization of Thatcher and Reagan, while recognizing and entrenching the accompanying social changes. However, they did not believe in limited government; on the contrary, they saw an activist, often expanded, role for government in helping individuals and families respond to the resulting challenges, while at the same time seeking to use market mechanisms to improve public services.

This approach was successful economically and electorally for a time – and it was very attractive for economists like me, who broadly think that markets do a good job of allocating resources, but that a proactive government is necessary to expand opportunity and reduce inequality. But it, too, seems to have reached its limits, particularly in the financial crisis and subsequent recession. This challenged the view that globalization could be successfully managed through light-touch and market-based mechanisms, while also making it much harder for governments to finance public services and social benefits.

Instead, the most successful political movements at the moment, whether in government or opposition, seem to rely little on either classical conservatism or liberalism: the defining feature of Germany's Angela Merkel, Europe's most successful 21st-century politician, was pragmatism, while populist groups such as the French Front National and the US Tea Party movement, offer an ill-defined reaction against capitalism or at least some of its contemporary manifestations.

The condensed idea
Freedom and markets versus order and tradition

26 Socialism

s socialism the opposite of capitalism? In one fundamental sense, it is. If capitalism is a system where the means of production, distribution and exchange are privately owned and controlled, and where decisions on what to produce are taken by those private owners, then socialism is a system where the means of production are owned and controlled by the workers.

Needless to say, the common criterion for socialism given above begs a number of questions. Who are the workers, and what do they own and how? A socialist system could, under this definition, be anything from one where all productive capacity was owned by the state (as was more or less the case in most of the countries of the Eastern bloc until 1989, and remains mostly the case in Cuba). Or it could be one where enterprises were owned directly by the people who worked in them, as was the vision of the cooperative movement. Or, as early socialist theorists proposed, ownership could be vested in local communities, who would collectively own and manage land and enterprises, but still trade with the outside world in the market.

Early attempts

The first practical experiments in socialism followed this last model. Robert Owen, who managed mills in New Lanark near Glasgow, introduced an eight-hour day and the first infants' school in Britain, although the underlying ownership model remained capitalist. In 1825, he established a fully socialist community at New Harmony in the United States, with money replaced by 'labour tickets'. It was to be short-lived; the enterprises were poorly managed and governance of the community was chaotic. A number of other similar experiments were tried, mostly in the US, but none proved durable.

After the failure of a series of revolutions across Europe in 1848, and the repression that followed, the idea that it was possible to create a socialist society from the ground up seemed much less plausible, and so those who sought workers' control moved to the political arena. The International Workingmen's Association, or First International, was founded in 1864 by Marx and others. Its objective was to take control of the state, either peacefully or violently, in order to establish socialism.

The Soviet experiment

The first avowedly socialist government came to power in Russia in 1917. This was a far less industrialized society than those of Western Europe, and therefore one far less suited to socialism according to Marx's theories (see Chapter 27). But the Bolsheviks moved quickly, first to put industry, and then agriculture, into government control and ownership. Under their central planning scheme, a state agency (called Gosplan) set output targets for every enterprise in the country. Instead of production being determined by privately owned businesses responding to market forces and incentives in order to maximize their returns, the planners would decide what society could produce and, given overall priorities, what it should produce.

This central planning model of socialism was extended to the countries of Eastern Europe under Soviet domination after 1945, and was also independently adopted by China under Mao. But it

> A socialist is just someone who is unable to get over his or her astonishment that most people who have lived and died have spent lives of wretched, fruitless, unremitting toil.
> Terry Eagleton, Professor of English Literature, Lancaster University

proved to be a resounding failure. While central planning might succeed in accelerating the rapid industrialization of a predominantly agrarian society (albeit at enormous human cost, as in Russia between the wars), it simply did not deliver either growth or prosperity in peacetime.

A flawed model

There were two main problems; first, without the balancing mechanism of supply and demand, shortages of some goods (and overproduction of others) was inevitable. Second, and even more fundamental was the lack of incentives for workers to be productive, for managers to maximize production and to maintain quality, and for anybody to seek to innovate or improve. Indeed, the only real incentive, at all levels, was to cheat in one way or another – by shirking at work, falsifying production figures, or producing, buying and selling on the many black markets that inevitably arose. In the words of a well-known Soviet joke, 'We pretend to work, and they pretend to pay us'.

The economic failure of central planning became more obvious in the 1970s and 1980s. Even prior to the collapse of the Soviet bloc in 1989, it led to interest in less centralized approaches that reintroduced the role of the market and incentives. The most thorough-going of these was the Yugoslav system of 'decentralized self-management', but this was little more effective, creating high inflation and foreign debt, and did not survive the dissolution of Yugoslavia itself. The largely agricultural Israeli kibbutz movement is perhaps the best-known example of a widespread, economically successful, socialist approach to production at a community and enterprise level, but even at its peak it did not represent more than a fraction of the Israeli economy.

> Socialism is a philosophy of failure, the creed of ignorance, and the gospel of envy, its inherent virtue is the equal sharing of misery.
> Winston Churchill

With the collapse of the Soviet bloc, the number of states that now adopt an avowedly socialist approach to the overall organization of the economy is tiny. While China still describes its extremely successful system as 'socialism with Chinese characteristics', the 'socialism' part refers more to the continued primacy of the Communist Party than any approach to economic management, as more and more of the economy moves into private hands. In advanced economies, meanwhile, there are numerous successful enterprises that incorporate some elements of socialist or cooperative principles – from Mondragon in the Basque country to the John Lewis Partnership in the UK, credit unions in the financial sector and numerous agricultural cooperatives. But all of these function within economies that are primarily capitalist. The idea of socialism as a fully fledged economic system appears to have run its course.

Einstein on socialism

It may be hard for us to credit now, but immediately after the Second World War, the 'planned economy' appeared to be a credible or even superior alternative to capitalism. This opinion was shared even among extremely intelligent people who by no means shared the politics of Stalin and the Russian leadership:

'The economic anarchy of capitalist society as it exists today is, in my opinion, the real source of the evil. I am convinced there is only one way to eliminate these grave evils, namely through the establishment of a socialist economy, accompanied by an educational system that would be oriented towards social goals. In such an economy, the means of production are owned by society itself and are utilized in a planned fashion. A planned economy, which adjusts production to the needs of the community, would distribute the work to be done among all those able to work and would guarantee a livelihood to every man, woman and child. The education of the individual, in addition to promoting his own innate abilities, would attempt to develop in him a sense of responsibility for his fellow men in place of the glorification of power and success in our present society.'
Albert Einstein

The condensed idea
Putting the workers in charge

27 Marxism

Marxism is widely, and rightly in my view, perceived as a largely failed ideology, defeated by capitalism both politically and economically. Yet ironically, whether we realize it or not, no one has contributed more to our understanding of capitalism than Karl Marx. Indeed, time and time again while writing this book I find myself referring back, knowingly or otherwise, to basic concepts first introduced by Marx.

Marx had two fundamental insights, the first of which was into the importance of economic forces in shaping human society. For Marx, it was the 'mode of production' – how labour and capital are combined, and under what rules – that explained more or less everything else about society. Politics, social relations, culture and so on were all rooted in this, and so as modes of production progress, develop and change, society does too:

> 'In the social production of their existence, men inevitably enter into definite relations, which are independent of their will, namely relations of production appropriate to a given stage in the development of their material forces of production. The totality of these relations of production constitutes the economic structure of society, the real foundation, on which arises a legal and political superstructure and to which correspond definite forms of social consciousness.'

From this belief, Marx correctly concluded that industrialization and capitalism would lead to profound changes in the nature of society, affecting everything from the political system to morality:

> 'All fixed, fast-frozen relations, with their train of ancient and venerable prejudices and opinions, are swept away, all new-formed ones become antiquated before they can ossify. All that is solid melts into air, all that is holy is profaned, and man is at last compelled to face with sober senses his real conditions of life, and his relations with his kind.'

Marx's second key insight was into the dynamic nature of capitalism itself. He understood that capitalism could not be static; the pursuit of the profit motive in a competitive economy meant that there would be constant pressure to increase the capital stock and improve productivity through technological progress. This in turn would lead to labour-saving, or capital-intensive, technological change. Later thinkers like Schumpeter developed this, introducing the concept of creative destruction (see Chapter 10). Putting these two insights together gives a picture of capitalism as a radical force. Its own internal dynamics mean that the economy is constantly evolving and changing, and this in turn results in changes in the wider society.

Marx's fundamental mistakes

What then did Marx get wrong? First, while he was correct that competition would lead the owners of capital to invest in productivity-enhancing – and labour-saving – machinery, he was wrong in thinking that this would lead to wages being driven down to subsistence level, as they had largely been under feudalism. In fact classical economics – which argued that new, higher productivity jobs would emerge, and that workers would, over time, see their wages rise more or less in line with productivity – got this one right.

And this in turn meant that Marx's most important political prediction – the inevitable conflict between workers and capitalists, leading in the end to the victory of the former and the abolition of capitalism – was wrong. Marx was correct that as the number of industrial workers rose they would demand their share of the wealth; and that, in contrast to feudalism, their number and geographical concentration in factories and big cities would mean that these demands could not be indefinitely denied. But the increased productivity generated by capitalism meant that in most advanced capitalist economies, the demands of the workers could be satisfied without the system itself collapsing. Indeed, so far at least, it seems that increased productivity, increased wages and hence increased

> Our judgment and moral categories, our idea of the future, our opinions about the present or about justice, peace, or war, everything, without excluding our rejections of Marxism, is impregnated with Marxism.
> Octavio Paz, Poet

consumption go hand in hand, not just in individual countries but worldwide (see Chapter 46).

Hence, while the rise of trade unions and universal suffrage meant that the exploitation foreseen by Marx was politically unsustainable, it also became economically unnecessary. Indeed, the economic benefits that largely capitalist systems delivered were sufficiently large that for most workers, they were preferable to the alternative. Where Marx's political ideas did triumph, it was largely as a consequence of the instability generated by war (as in Russia), or in agrarian pre-industrial societies where versions of feudalism persisted (like China and Vietnam). Where the 'Marxist' leaders of these countries tried to introduce industrialization without capitalism, they failed – a failure that, ironically, Marx would probably have predicted.

The inevitable crisis of capitalism

On one big question, however, the jury remains out. Marx argued that capitalism was inherently subject to crises – booms and busts, generated by the overaccumulation of capital, overproduction, falls in the rate of profit and hence an inevitable crash. Over time, these cycles would become larger and more destabilizing, until eventually the system would destroy itself as a consequence of its own internal dynamics.

Keynes and Friedman both took this challenge seriously, and explained how macroeconomic management, using fiscal and monetary policy, could dampen economic cycles. Hence, until recently, the majority of economists thought that they had indeed solved the problem of boom and bust, or at least made it manageable. The global financial crisis of 2008–9 (and the fact that we still do not fully understand why it occurred or, more importantly, the risks of it happening again) call that into question.

So will Marx have the last laugh after all? That is, does the dynamic nature of capitalism mean that crises will continue, and indeed become larger and more global, until eventually the system itself becomes unsustainable? So far, capitalism has been remarkably resilient, and my prediction – for what it's worth – is that we'll still be analysing it, using Marx's insights, for the foreseeable future.

The end of history?

After the fall of the Berlin Wall, some liberal historians and political analysts argued that we had reached the 'end of history' – that is, that Western-style liberal democracy was now the only viable form of government. This was a deliberate, and somewhat triumphalist, inversion of Marx's view that the 'end of history' would be the replacement of liberal democracy by communism.

> 'What we may be witnessing is not just the end of the Cold War, or the passing of a particular period of post-war history, but the end of history as such: that is, the end point of mankind's ideological evolution and the universalization of Western liberal democracy as the final form of human government.'
> *Francis Fukuyama*

Marx would have had little patience with this. He might (grudgingly, I suspect) concede that his predictions that the industrial proletariat would become a unified and dominant political force were mistaken. But he would have pointed to globalization and its crises, and the transformative and destabilizing nature of technological advance, and he would have concluded that 'liberal capitalism' was itself a passing historical moment. On the whole, events since 1989 have largely borne this out – liberal democracy is still alive and (more or less) well, but it is by no means triumphant everywhere, either economically or politically.

The condensed idea
History is economics

28 The Keynesian revolution

I f markets are working properly, supply and demand should be equal: the price mechanism will take care of that. This fundamental principle seems to work pretty well for most simple goods. But does it work for the whole economy? Can supply and demand be out of balance overall? And if so, what, if anything, should the government do about it?

This question was posed and answered by the French economist Jean-Baptiste Say, who coined what has become known as Say's Law:

'A product is no sooner created, than it, from that instant, affords a market for other products to the full extent of its own value. As each of us can only purchase the productions of others with his own productions – as the value we can buy is equal to the value we can produce, the more men can produce, the more they will purchase.'

In other words, 'supply creates its own demand'. This proposition has important implications. In particular, it means that there cannot be overproduction at the level of the economy as a whole, or a general glut of goods. So the level of economic activity simply depends on the capacity of the economy to produce: if there's unemployment or recession, then either it's due to some external shock, or it's the result of government intervention in the economy (for example, paying unemployment benefits).

Say's Law was controversial at the time, with John Stuart Mill arguing that the existence of money meant that supply and demand need not balance overall. But it justified the 'laissez-faire' approach to economic management that prevailed throughout the 19th century. If the economy as a whole naturally tends to an equilibrium, then government intervention in the economy may occasionally be necessary, but it is a necessary evil. And it certainly cannot deal with the causes or consequences of recessions, since these are not really an economic phenomenon.

In particular, trying to boost demand and hence employment by increasing government spending is pointless. After all, the money has to come from somewhere (either from taxation or from borrowing) and if the government spends it, someone else in the private sector cannot. So government spending and borrowing (fiscal policy) cannot affect aggregate demand or employment.

Keynes and the Depression

It was the Great Depression of the 1930s that led to a reappraisal. In the UK, with unemployment soaring, the 'Treasury View' – in essence Say's Law under another guise – was used to justify the government's decision to ignore the advice of John Maynard Keynes and others to increase spending.

Perhaps the central objective of Keynes' 1936 magnum opus – *The General Theory of Employment, Interest and Money* – was to comprehensively dismantle the intellectual basis for Say's Law. Keynes argued that while in the long run, supply and demand would indeed tend to balance at the aggregate level, the 'long run' was not a very helpful concept:

> 'But this long run is a misleading guide to current affairs. In the long run we are all dead. Economists set themselves too easy, too useless a task, if in tempestuous seasons they can only tell us, that when the storm is long past, the ocean is flat again.'

Keynes argued that in the short run, demand rather than supply was the key driver of economic activity, and in very broad terms this is what economists mean by 'Keynesianism'. If, for whatever reason, the private sector collectively wanted to save more than it collectively wanted to invest, there would be a problem; since overall savings have to equal overall investment, something would have to adjust, and the result would be a fall in income and output. Contrary to the Treasury View then, government spending, if financed by borrowing, would increase both income and output, because it would give a home to the extra saving. This would be true even if the spending was not particularly productive.

Keynes was not always clear on when and whether the appropriate form of government intervention was fiscal policy (government spending and borrowing) or monetary policy (the level of interest

> If the Treasury were to fill old bottles with banknotes, bury them at suitable depths in disused coalmines ... and leave it to private enterprise on well-tried principles of laissez-faire to dig the notes up again, there need be no more unemployment and, with the help of the repercussions, the real income of the community ... would probably become a good deal greater than it actually is.
>
> John Maynard Keynes

rates). But the principle that governments can and should manage the economy at an aggregate level, with the aim of both preventing and mitigating recessions, became the central aim of post-war economic management in capitalist economies. President Richard Nixon said 'We are all Keynesians now', and in the 1950s and 1960s governments actively managed the economy to minimize unemployment.

However, in the 1970s, Keynesianism as practised seemed to break down, as stabilizing unemployment began to require higher and higher levels of inflation. It was first replaced by monetarism, propounded by Milton Friedman (who argued that monetary policy was preferable to fiscal policy as a tool of macroeconomic management – see Chapter 16). Ultimately, ideas from both Keynes and Friedman were incorporated into the 'neoclassical synthesis'. While the principle that it was the government's responsibility to manage the overall economy remained, there was a much greater degree of scepticism about how effective this was likely to be. Keynes remained out of fashion, while in academic economics, the last two decades saw something of a revival of Say's Law, under the guise of 'Real Business Cycle Theory', which claimed that neither monetary nor fiscal policy could really make much difference, even in the short run. However, hardly anyone in the real world believed this.

The return of Keynesianism?

The global financial crisis of 2008–9 reopened the debate. Suddenly monetary policy seemed impotent, and there was a resurgence of interest in old-fashioned fiscal Keynesianism. For better or worse, the Great Recession has revived the view that without active government intervention, economies can get stuck in long periods of high unemployment and low or no growth – even if there is no consensus at all on what they should do about it.

Keynes and the Great Financial Crisis

At the April 2009 G20 Conference in London, the leaders of the world's largest economies announced the 'largest fiscal and monetary stimulus' in modern times. Yet, only a year later, with the world economy recovering, the International Monetary Fund recommended a 'pivot' to fiscal consolidation, and many countries announced deficit reduction and austerity programmes. With global growth since then deeply disappointing, does this mean Keynesianism worked, and we should have had more of it; or that it should never have been tried at all? The arguments rage on, among both economists and politicians. Nobel Prizewinner Eugene Fama argued against President Obama's stimulus package:

'Bailouts and stimulus plans are funded by issuing more government debt. The added debt absorbs savings that would otherwise go to private investment. In the end, despite the existence of idle resources, bailouts and stimulus plans do not add to current resources in use.'

My view, however, is that of Keynes. As Paul Krugman put it:

'If we discovered that space aliens were planning to attack, and we needed a massive build-up to counter the space alien threat, and inflation and budget deficits took secondary place to that, this slump would be over in 18 months.'

The condensed idea
Supply doesn't always match demand

29 Nationalization and privatization

Between the 14th and 17th centuries, the largest industrial enterprise in Europe, possibly the world, was the Arsenale of Venice, whose ships formed the basis for the city's naval power. Throughout history, such strategic parts of the economy, in particular communications and facilities that produce munitions, were owned and controlled by the state.

In the period before the Industrial Revolution, state ownership generally reflected considerations of power, not economics. The idea that the state should own productive enterprises that produce goods for use and consumption in the market was a much later conception. Broadly, there were three rationales for the wave of nationalizations undertaken in most Western economies (but not, for the most part, the United States) after the Second World War:

• That set out in Clause IV of the Constitution of the British Labour Party, 1918–95: 'To secure for the workers by hand or by brain the full fruits of their industry and the most equitable distribution thereof that may be possible upon the basis of the common ownership of the means of production, distribution and exchange, and the best obtainable system of popular administration and control of each industry or service'. In other words, in societies that remained primarily capitalist and where most productive activity remained within the market sector, nationalization of some of the largest firms was seen as a way of limiting the power of capital and redistributing its proceeds, both with respect to workers in those industries, and society at large. (It's worth noting, however, that despite Clause IV, the Labour Party never seriously sought to overthrow capitalism itself).
• The view that state ownership and control of strategic industries such as coal, steel and shipbuilding was necessary in order to plan the post-war economic reconstruction and development of the shattered countries of Western Europe.
• The fact that many utilities – the electricity, water, rail, gas and telephone sectors – were 'natural monopolies'. This meant that they

required large amounts of investment, which could most efficiently be provided by the public sector, and also that if left in private hands, their monopoly status was likely to lead to overcharging of consumers.

Nationalization and nationalism

For some developing countries, nationalization was also a way of returning natural resources, particularly oil, to domestic control. The 1938 nationalization of the oil industry in Mexico was an important event in the country's assertion of economic independence from the US, while in Iran, the US and UK infamously arranged a 1953 coup against the democratically elected prime minister to prevent nationalization of the Anglo–Persian oil company.

But all of these rationales weakened over the post-war period. Planning that had been essential to reconstruction became less and less relevant. And while the idea had been that nationalized industries, free from the whims of markets, would be able to invest for the long term, they were instead subject to the whims of politicians, which often turned out to be extremely short term. In particular, trade unions became especially powerful in nationalized industries, and often used that power (understandably, but ultimately damagingly) to protect the short-term interests of their members at the expense of the public who ultimately financed the industries.

> When you take into public ownership a profitable industry the profits soon disappear. The goose that laid the golden eggs goes broody. State geese are not great layers.
> Margaret Thatcher

There were exceptions, such as Norway's Statoil, but overall the economic performance of nationalized industries was disappointing. And, crucially, the case for nationalized public utilities was weakened both by technology and by advances in the economics of regulation, which proposed ways in which private firms could be given incentives to operate efficiently without being allowed monopoly profits.

Privatization

Nationalized industries performed particularly badly in Britain, and it was here that the wave of privatizations began in the 1980s. Electricity, gas, telephones, water, steel, airlines and more were all returned to the private sector, usually by selling shares to the public and private markets. Other countries followed suit, albeit more patchily, and the privatization movement was given renewed vigour by the fall of communism, as many formerly communist countries sought to privatize state-owned enterprises.

In general, privatization does seem to have achieved the objective of improving economic efficiency, particularly in firms in competitive markets; Lufthansa and British Airways, both privatized, have generally performed rather better than state-owned European airlines like Alitalia or Olympic Airways. Particularly in telecommunications, technological change has made the idea of a single, monopoly, state-owned provider obsolete.

However, in industries where natural monopolies persist and competition is limited, the record is less clear. Water privatization has been a costly failure from consumers' perspective. Attempts to introduce competition to rail and electricity by separating out ownership of the network (the electricity grid or the rail lines) from direct provision of services to consumers (power supplies or train services) have had, at best, mixed results. Ironically, the electricity powering my computer today (in London) is supplied by EDF Energy, a state-owned French company, which is also planning to build a nuclear power station in the UK in partnership with a Chinese company. And I arrived at work on a bus run by Arriva, which is owned by the Germany state railway company Deutsche Bahn.

Despite this general trend, a dramatic recent wave of renationalizations was prompted not by ideology, but by the 2008–9 financial crisis. Countries across Europe nationalized, in whole or in part, much of their troubled banking sector. In the US, not only were the major mortgage providers nationalized, but the government took a controlling interest in General Motors, once the largest company in the country. Some of these moves have since been wholly or partially reversed, but they are a reminder that the move back towards private ownership is by no means inexorable; the state is still obliged to pick up the pieces when things go badly wrong.

I joined the Labour Party in 1983, just before its worst-ever election defeat. Its manifesto – famously described as the 'longest suicide note in history' – called for nationalization of huge swathes of British industry. A quarter century later, both the Labour Party and I had moved on. The former had long since abandoned nationalization as an instrument of economic policy, while I was Chief Economist at the Cabinet Office, and, as a civil servant, strictly politically neutral. And so it was that in October 2008, I found myself sitting in Number 10 Downing Street, with the Prime Minister, the Chancellor of the Exchequer and the Governor of the Bank of England as they decided that in order to prevent the collapse of the UK financial system, and perhaps capitalism itself, it was necessary to nationalize most of the British banking system – something that even the 1983 Labour Party had not contemplated.

The condensed idea
Governments aren't good at running businesses

30 The Welfare State

Social structures that helped the sick, the poor and the old existed before capitalism. But they were generally local and based on charity of one sort or another, from the better off or via the Church. However, urbanization, industrialization and rapid economic growth meant that new structures were required for a number of reasons.

In economies that were largely rural, and where both population and economic growth were slow, reliance on a very basic charitable system was sustainable both economically and socially, and was seen by most as inevitable. At times of economic crisis or famine, rulers often organized distributions of food, sometimes combined with make-work schemes to provide employment. But none of this prevented poverty and severe hardship being widespread in almost all societies, almost all the time; in every pre-industrial society, a large proportion of the population died prematurely, as a direct or indirect consequence of poverty.

With the coming of industrialization, however, an alternative was needed. Marx hypothesized that the logic of capitalism meant that, since individual capitalists would seek to maximize their surpluses, they would pay workers the absolute minimum, keeping them at, or near, subsistence level. Eventually, workers would find this state of affairs so intolerable that, peacefully or violently, they would overthrow the system. But political developments took a rather different turn. Workers did indeed organize – but in the first instance they sought better pay and conditions, and, crucially, provision by employers or the state for sickness, unemployment and old age, rather than direct ownership of industry. And employers (and the governments they directly or indirectly controlled) eventually responded. They feared industrial unrest, and, perhaps, revolution; and the more far-sighted ones at least recognized that a relatively healthy and prosperous workforce was also good for demand.

The first major national programmes of social insurance were introduced not in Britain (where trade unions concentrated their efforts on improving working conditions, but were politically weak) but by the architect of German reunification, Otto von Bismarck. While this was partly to head off the political threat of the world's largest workers' party, the Social Democratic Party, it also served the interests of German industry – emigration to the United States fell sharply. Other European countries largely followed suit, although everywhere many people remained uncovered, and much provision was through unions or other 'mutualist' associations rather than the state itself.

Post-war growth

The Great Depression illustrated the inadequacy of existing welfare provision, and the post-war period saw the establishment of comprehensive welfare states as we now know them in almost every industrialized country. It is important to remember, however, that redistribution – taking money from the better off to give it to the less well off – was neither the original purpose of the welfare state, nor is it its main function today. From an economic perspective, the welfare state in fact has three key functions:

> Over time, the welfare state has become dysfunctional in a surprising way. But in a way it became a victim of its own success: It became so successful at prolonging life, that it becomes financially unsustainable, unless you make major changes to things like retirement ages.
> Niall Ferguson

• Old-age provision, which is generally the largest single item of state spending in most developed countries, may partly redistribute money from rich to poor, but it is mostly about transferring money from young workers to retired ones. Since most of us will be in both situations over our lives, this can be seen as a system of forced saving for retirement.

• Insurance against involuntary unemployment, or that caused by ill-health or disability. Again, this is more about sharing risk than redistribution.

• There is a truly redistributive component to welfare in most countries, but it is much smaller than the headline figures, and usually driven not so much by how welfare money is spent, but by how it is raised (through taxes that take more from those with higher incomes).

Most countries have some form of provision for children as well, which can reflect a number of purposes. It functions as 'insurance' against the loss of earnings power from looking after children, serves the interest of the economy as a whole in ensuring that people continue to reproduce, and prevents severe hardship among the children of those who are not working or earning enough. In almost all countries, with the notable exception (until recently at least) of the United States, access to healthcare is also regarded as a key element of the welfare state.

The future of the welfare state

Over the last decade, the death of the welfare state has been announced frequently, both by the political left and the right. The right makes at least three arguments against it:

• **It is unnecessary** After all, private markets can provide insurance against foreseeable contingencies like old age (there are plenty of private pension providers) and ill health (the government merely needs to ensure the health insurance markets are working).

• **It is unaffordable** Demographic changes mean we will have more pensioners and fewer workers, and technological change makes healthcare ever more expensive.

• **It is damaging** Excessive welfare reduces the incentive to work.

On the left, meanwhile, it is easy to find those who think not only that individual changes to welfare provision are damaging, but that the welfare state itself is being destroyed wherever there is a right-wing or even centrist government.

However, neither of these perspectives is remotely realistic. Although countries will continue to have a mix of private and public provision for old-age pensions, governments will largely determine what this provision looks like. The same goes for healthcare; even in the US, government spending on healthcare is 8 per cent of GDP. In the UK, under a Conservative-led government, recent years have seen major cutbacks in some areas of welfare provision, causing severe hardship, but the overall proportion of government spending on welfare, health and education has never been higher. Demographics and technological change pose major challenges to the financing and organization of the welfare state, but as citizens that is likely to mean we will demand more, not less, help from the state in ensuring our future security in old age and ill health.

The condensed idea
Economic progress requires social cohesion

31 The Industrial Revolution

Until the middle of the 18th century, the vast majority of humanity was employed in agriculture and lived in rural areas. This had been the case for thousands of years, and there didn't seem to be any particular reason things should change. But somewhere around 1760, beginning in the United Kingdom, it did.

Although the population of pre-industrial Western Europe had been growing steadily since the 16th century, it was doing so quite slowly, and there was no consistent or sustained growth in per capita income. Malnutrition and disease were, as they always had been, pretty much a constant, and for most of the population, life was nasty, brutish and frequently short. There was certainly no reason to take for granted, as we do today, the notion of economic 'progress' or growth. Change, when it came, was triggered by the introduction of new production processes. In particular, the mechanization of manufacturing transformed, first the British, and then the world economy. This led to unprecedented growth, both of the economy and the population; to urbanization; and, eventually, to a sustained growth in living standards for the vast majority of the population.

The steam age

The key innovations of the Industrial Revolution were steam power (which enabled mechanization by providing a power source that could drive a factory) and a succession of inventions that made use of it. These included the spinning frame and power loom, which transformed the production of textiles from a household or cottage industry to an industrial process carried out in large factories. But a whole host of other interlocking developments were important. Improvements in iron smelting and casting made it easier to produce agricultural machinery, which in turn freed up agricultural labour to work in factories. Meanwhile, the development of transport infrastructure, such as roads, canals and railways, enabled goods to be brought to market more easily.

Just as these technological developments still influence how we live today, their economic, political and social consequences still shape contemporary capitalism. Industrialization both required capitalism, and facilitated its development. In contrast to a largely agricultural economy, building factories required huge investment, and company law and the financial system needed to adapt to make this possible. As agriculture became more efficient, workers migrated to cities, providing labour for factories. Competition was fierce, particularly to invent and develop new and more productive machines and processes. Rewards for successful entrepreneurs were substantial.

> The Industrial Revolution was a watershed in the history of mankind. Three forces – technology, economic organization and science, in this sequence – each from separate and undistinguished parentage, linked up ... to form, hardly a hundred years ago, into a social maelstrom that is still engulfing new and new millions of people, in an irresistible rush.
>
> Karl Polanyi

Political implications

And just as industrialization required capitalism, capitalism in turn led ultimately to democracy. Economic and political power shifted from the landed aristocracy to the new capitalist class of industrialists and businessmen, and from the countryside to the cities. This in turn meant that governments pursued policies that facilitated further growth of industry. In Britain, for example, the repeal of Corn Laws that imposed heavy tariffs on imported grain made domestic agriculture less profitable, but at the same time as making food more affordable for urban workers.

The rise of factory-produced goods meant that ordinary people had access to more and better products than ever before. An average 18th-century Briton would have probably had one or two shirts; factory production made them affordable for almost everybody. Famine and malnutrition were much less prevalent in cities than they had been in rural areas, and while there is still controversy over the precise causes and responsibility for the Irish Potato Famine of 1845–49, the fact that it happened in largely rural and agrarian Ireland, rather than industrializing England, clearly reflected the imbalance in economic strength and political power. Ireland continued to export food to England, mostly to feed England's growing urban population, throughout the famine.

But conditions for workers during the early industrial period, even if preferable to a rural existence, were still dreadful. Richard Arkwright, who invented the spinning frame, arguably pioneered the modern factory system. His employees, including children as young as seven, worked 13-hour days in frequently dangerous conditions, and accidents, including fatal ones, were common. Living conditions were tough, too: cities like Manchester and Bradford grew too rapidly for housing and sanitation to keep pace, so they became polluted and disease-ridden.

But, over time, as workers organized themselves economically and politically, they captured a greater share of the economic benefits of industrialization. Real wages and living standards increased, especially after around 1830. Despite the objections of free-market purists, working conditions were regulated, with the introduction of limits on working time and restrictions on child labour.

Industrialization quickly spread to other countries. By the end of the 19th century, the US had become the world's leading industrial power. The urbanization that resulted also spurred both technological change and an increased role for government. The big advances in the quality of life for ordinary people began in the latter half of the 19th century, first with the introduction of modern water and sewerage systems, and then electricity and public transport – all of which enabled further urbanization in what is sometimes referred to as the second Industrial Revolution. Between 1851 and 1891, London's population rose from just over 2 million to more than 5 million.

Most of the key legal and political institutions and structures that underlie what we think of as modern capitalist society – companies and stock markets, trade unions and the welfare state, even representative democracy – are directly or indirectly a result of the Industrial Revolution, and the forms of economic organization that it necessitated. But today few of us work in factories, and mass manufacturing is a dwindling share of most Western economies. Moreover, advances in information and communication technology are already beginning to transform the shape of the economy further, and this process has arguably only just begun. Whether or not we call this another Industrial Revolution, its implications will be economic and social, just as much as technological. And the changes in store could be just as profound as those we saw in the 19th century.

Why did the Industrial Revolution take place in Britain, and why in the mid-18th century? We're still not sure, but the long period of (domestic) peace and stability following the unification of Scotland and England in 1707, the relatively large domestic market with no internal trade barriers, and a legal system that was both reasonably stable and reliable, and able to adapt to the requirements of a changing economy all certainly helped. Similar circumstances had come together in other countries before, however, without such dramatic results. More controversial is the contribution made by Britain's colonial empire: as a source of profits (especially from slave plantations in the Caribbean), a source of raw materials and a captive market for manufactured goods (especially in India, where the British deliberately suppressed domestic production of textiles).

The condensed idea
Humanity's great take-off

32 Imperialism and colonialism

Empires existed long before the development of capitalism, some driven by power politics, and some by the will to exploit a variety of resources found in other parts of the world. Yet, despite this, it's clear that the 'Age of Empires' in the 19th and early 20th centuries coincided with the spread of capitalism.

There was nothing particularly 'capitalist' about the Roman Empire: the Romans conquered other peoples and territory, and incorporated and retained them in an empire by military force. The empire then provided law and order and protection from external threat, which facilitated economic development, but not of a specifically capitalist character. More purely exploitative empires, such as the Spanish Empire, were primarily directed at extracting resources (especially silver and gold) for the benefit of the ruling class of the conquering countries. This had little or nothing to do directly with the accumulation of physical capital necessary for capitalist development, particularly since silver and gold were non-productive assets.

The Age of Imperialism

However, it was hardly a coincidence that the development of modern capitalism in the United Kingdom in the 19th century coincided with the vast expansion of the British Empire, as well as imperialist ventures by other emerging capitalist powers (including Belgium, France, Germany, and the United States to a limited extent) – the Age of Imperialism.

One view, advanced (in part) by Marx and later by Lenin, was that capitalism required imperialism. Since the logic of capitalism was that productive capacity would outpace consumer demand, there would be no profitable domestic opportunities, and investment would have to look abroad. Since all industrializing countries would share the same problem, this would only be possible if new countries were absorbed into the system (forcibly or otherwise). The 19th century did seem to bear this out, at least for the UK; the new manufacturing industries did indeed generate huge trade surpluses, requiring large

The textile trade

Perhaps the most powerful example of the interaction between imperialism and capitalism was that of the textile trade between Britain and India. Before the Industrial Revolution, India was by far the largest producer of textiles, and – with trade under the control of the East India Company – exported considerable quantities to Britain. But over the following century, patterns of trade shifted radically. Instead of cotton being farmed, spun, woven, dyed and manufactured into cloth in India, it was farmed in the US – using slave labour – and shipped to the UK where the new factories turned it into machine-made yarn and then cloth, which was both consumed in the UK and exported to the captive Indian market. The Indian textile industry was largely destroyed.

The precise role of UK trade policy – both in encouraging exports to India, and in protecting the British market with tariffs on imported goods – is still disputed. Certainly by the middle of the 19th century the UK textile industry, as a consequence of the wave of innovation unleashed by capitalist development, was far more efficient than the non-mechanized Indian one, and no longer needed the direct support of trade policy. (Equally, it survived the abolition of slavery in the US.) But there is little doubt that if the UK had not been ruling India throughout the period, things would have been very different. And the destruction of the domestic textile industry had a lasting impact on both political and economic developments in India as well.

amounts of foreign investment, although not all flowed to countries that were formally part of the British Empire.

The interaction between the political and military aspects of imperialism and the economic ones was always key. Imperial Preference, a system of preferential tariffs for the countries of the empire, was designed both to promote political unity within the empire and to sustain the United Kingdom's position as a global mercantile power in response to the rise of Germany and the United States. But while empire was popular in Britain, protectionism, and the consequent increase in prices for working class consumers, was not. Hence, Imperial Preference was abandoned before the start of the Second World War.

Decolonization

J.A. Hobson, an English economist whose work formed the basis for Lenin's theories, had earlier pointed out that if domestic demand kept pace with productive capacity, the natural tendency of capitalism towards imperial expansion could be kept in check.

And indeed, after the Second World War, decolonization and the dismantling of empires proceeded alongside a new phase of capitalist development. With more of the pie going to wages than capital, the proceeds of growth were shared domestically, so that domestic demand grew roughly in line with productive capacity in most advanced economies. The UK, for example, has never consistently run a balance of payments surplus since then.

> In order to save the forty million inhabitants of the United Kingdom from a bloody civil war, our colonial statesmen must acquire new lands for settling the surplus population of this country, to provide new markets ... The Empire, as I have always said, is a bread and butter question.
>
> Cecil Rhodes

The economic importance of imperial connections dwindled accordingly. Although they remained important in some respects (until the 1990s, most post-war immigrants to the United Kingdom and France came from those countries' former imperial possessions), this was not true of trade. The UK abandoned the last vestiges of Imperial Preference when it joined the European Economic Community, and it now trades considerably less with India than it does with Belgium.

Imperialism per se is not a feature of the current international order: even when more powerful countries invade less powerful ones, the primary motivation is generally not economic. Afghanistan is unlikely to become a significant market for the US anytime soon; and even though Iraq has very large oil reserves, no rational cost-benefit analysis would suggest that invasion has resulted in anything other than very large economic costs (although of course some specific companies and sectors have done very well indeed). The United States, in particular, much prefers to pursue its economic interests in resource-rich countries (such as the oil-producing states of the Gulf) by co-opting local elites rather than by the direct use of force.

Neocolonialism

But this does not mean that international imbalances in power relations no longer impact economic developments. The theory of 'neo-colonialism' emerged to describe how, even without direct political or military control, advanced capitalist countries use political and economic influence to ensure that less developed countries continue to serve as a cheap source of raw materials, and a ready market. There is some force to this argument, as the history of the Democratic Republic of the Congo since decolonization shows; it has been continually interfered with and fought over by foreign powers, from within Africa and beyond, in large part because of its mineral wealth.

> If it were necessary to give the briefest possible definition of imperialism, we should have to say that imperialism is the monopoly stage of capitalism.
> Lenin

But this type of direct exploitation of very poor countries is now more the exception than the rule. Perhaps more damaging is the way the most developed countries seek to use their economic strength to ensure that the rules of international trade benefit their domestic industries. For example, the US has devoted considerable effort to stopping the production of cheap generic drugs, often made in India, in order to benefit its own drug manufacturers. Even during the coronavirus pandemic, advanced economies still put the interests of their manufacturers first. Fairer and freer trade would benefit all of us.

The condensed idea
The economics of exploitation

33 War

'**N**o two countries that both had McDonald's have fought a war against each other since each got its McDonald's.' So claimed columnist Thomas Friedman. Is there something unique about capitalism that prevents, or at least strongly discourages, armed conflict between capitalist countries?

Friedman, writing in the *New York Times* in 1999, called his observation the 'Golden Arches Theory of Conflict Prevention'. His argument was explicitly based on the thesis that capitalist development would reduce and ultimately eliminate war, because, once a country had reached a sufficient level of development to provide an attractive market for McDonald's, that would indicate that it had developed a sufficiently large, and economically powerful, middle class for war to be against the economic interests of the majority of the population.

Shortly afterwards, however, US warplanes bombed the Serbian capital Belgrade, which had since 1988 had several very popular McDonald's. Displaying a disheartening failure to appreciate the economic imperatives of capitalism and globalization, an angry mob attacked and set fire to them.

But Friedman's theory was hardly new. In 1909, Norman Angell's *The Great Illusion* argued that conquest was no longer economically beneficial:

> 'The incentive to produce [of the local population] would be sapped and the conquered area be rendered worthless. Thus, the conquering power had to leave property in the hands of the local population while incurring the costs of conquest and occupation.'

Capitalism made conquest unprofitable

In other words, prior to industrialization, a victorious military power could simply expropriate the physical assets (gold or treasure) or plunder the natural resources of a defeated one, or even use its population as slaves. Under capitalism, however, the wealth of a country depends on its productive capacity, and this cannot be simply confiscated – the sophistication of modern production techniques requires labour and expertise to produce wealth, and this in turn requires a measure of cooperation. War for the purposes of conquest is no longer a profitable proposition.

> The spirit of commerce ... sooner or later takes hold of every nation, and is incompatible with war.
> Immanuel Kant

Moreover, the rapid period of globalization around the turn of the 20th century, and the consequent economic interdependence between industrial countries, meant that war would be damaging to all countries involved. This followed directly from Adam Smith's argument that free trade benefited all participants – destroying the economy of another country would therefore not benefit the victor (by eliminating competitors) but, by reducing trade, harm all countries, including the victorious one. In 1913, *The Economist* published an editorial titled *War Becomes Impossible in Civilized World*:

> 'The powerful bonds of commercial interest between ourselves and Germany have been immensely strengthened in recent years ... removing Germany from the list of our possible foes.'

But of course capitalism did not stop conflict, and the Great War put an end to this optimism. War was clearly not in the long-term economic interests of the main protagonists (if anyone benefited, it was the US and Japan, who were relatively peripheral), but that did not stop it happening.

Burning ambition

The Second World War was followed by a long era of relative peace; while there were plenty of armed conflicts, people were actually less likely to die violently than in any other era of recorded history. But the era from 1945 to 1989 was also overshadowed by the perpetual risk of direct conflict between the Soviet bloc and NATO, and perhaps this threat of conflict was precisely what capitalism needed for economic stability and growth. It had been rearmament, after all, that finally pulled the US and Europe out of the Great Depression; and the Second World War itself that had eliminated unemployment. Following the war, the US in particular pursued an economic policy that has been described as 'militarized Keynesianism'; that is, it addressed the Marxist problem of overproduction and capitalism's need for ever expanding markets by the Keynesian solution of having government spend huge amounts on military equipment.

From this perspective, an all-out, hugely destructive war with the Soviet Union would have been disastrous; but the occasional limited war like Korea, Vietnam and the numerous US interventions in small Latin American countries to stave off the threat of communism were very useful in ensuring political support for high levels of military spending. President Dwight Eisenhower, a Republican and himself an ex-general, labelled this the 'military-industrial complex'. Moreover, since the military was always seeking technological improvements to weaponry, its spending generated technological advances that percolated into the wider economy. The Defense Advanced Research Projects Agency (DARPA), established in response to the Soviet launch of the first artificial satellite Sputnik 1, is generally regarded as having played an important role in developing the technologies that made the Internet possible.

Iraq was not a capitalist war

Ironically, it wasn't war that brought down the Soviet system – but the far better economic performance of capitalism. After the fall of communism, political support for high levels of military spending (and indeed for small wars) fell sharply in capitalist countries. While individual businessmen, often closely linked to the Bush administration, did indeed benefit considerably from the 2003 Iraq War, it's very difficult to see that it had anything other than a large cost for the US economy (Nobel Prizewinner Joseph Stiglitz put it at some $3 trillion). While the US and other countries are engaged in military action against the Islamic State, in scale and scope this hardly approaches the level of a war of any economic significance. And while the military-industrial complex remains politically important in the US, its economic weight is much reduced, from about 10 per cent of GDP in the 1950s and 1960s, to about 3.5 per cent today. So perhaps Friedman was right: capitalist countries would be crazy to go to war with each other, and while they will engage in limited military action to defend their citizens, anything remotely resembling the large-scale wars of the past will become ever more unlikely.

From the dawn of human history until 1945, Europe has been the site of more or less continuous armed conflict – wars, civil wars, massacres, religious terror, nationalist and separatist violence. Even during periods of relative peace, the threat of war or state violence was rarely far away. But war between any of Europe's constituent countries – especially the main historical protagonists, France, Germany, the UK, Italy and Spain – seemed, until the recent Ukraine conflict, almost unthinkable.

This, however, ignores the lessons of the Great War. The two largest capitalist economies in the world today – the US and China – are hugely interdependent. Neither, obviously, wishes to occupy the territory of the other, and while they compete in many markets, trade between the two is economically beneficial to both countries. From an economic perspective, military conflict can only be a losing proposition for both. But equally, their interests are not aligned everywhere, and they are already competing for power and influence in ways not dissimilar to the Great Powers of the early 20th century. Moreover, they will continue to seek to ensure military superiority through technological advance. War would undoubtedly be irrational, but history tells us that does not make it impossible.

The condensed idea
War is bad for business

34 Globalization

There's nothing remotely new about global trade. The ancient Silk Road wasn't a road, but a network, and trade in silk was far from its only or main function. From the time of Christ to the middle of the second millennium, it carried not only a wide variety of goods, but also led to the movement and interchange of people, cultures and ideas.

The rise of European empires from 1600 led to a growth in world trade, but not in the form that we know today: in contrast to the largely market-driven mutual exchange of the Silk Road, it was driven by the colonization of the Americas and imperial expansion in Asia, especially India. In the case of South America, the main flow was of precious metals back to Spain. But perhaps the most emblematic example of early modern globalization was the 'Triangular Trade': guns, gold and jewellery were shipped from Britain and other countries to Africa, where they were traded for slaves to be shipped to the Caribbean and the American colonies, who in turn produced cotton and tobacco to be sent back to Europe.

The rise and fall of the first wave of globalization

But it was a combination of the Industrial Revolution, mass migration and modern finance that permitted the first truly 'global' wave of globalization in the second half of the 19th century. The huge increase in the production of manufactured products meant that new markets were needed – and the invention of steamships meant that goods could be shipped far more rapidly and reliably. Railways, often financed by capital flows from the City of London, meant that goods could be transported to and from ports in the Americas and India. The latter, for example, had no railways in 1848; 30 years later it had 15,000 kilometres (9,000 miles). The UK was running a huge trade surplus from selling its manufactures to the world; to balance this, very large capital outflows were required, which financed UK investment from Argentina to India. And there were also huge flows of people, mostly from Europe to the Americas.

The First World War killed globalization in this form, and the era between the wars saw restrictions on trade, capital flows and migration. Following the Second World War, trade took a long time to recover, and capital flows were still highly regulated.

Rapid growth

The current era of globalization is also the product of both technological and political change. Key technological developments range from the spread of information and communications technologies to the containerization revolution in the transport of goods. Meanwhile, the end of the Bretton Woods system (see Chapter 16) and removal of capital controls in most industrialized countries, the fall of the Berlin Wall and, perhaps most of all, the decision of the Chinese leadership in 1979 to embark on a journey towards a market economy, have meant a huge reduction in barriers to trade and capital flows.

These changes meant that the period from 1980 to 2007 saw both trade and capital flows grow much faster than world output; in other words, a much higher proportion of what was produced was consumed in a different country, with the financial system recycling the resulting surpluses and financing the resulting deficits. Nor was this era of globalization just about trade in goods: for the first time, services, from telephone call centres to tourism and higher education, became an important component of world trade. Less tangible, but even more obvious, was the growth in interconnectedness of people and cultures, driven by the sharp fall in the price of communication, as English became the world's de facto international language and US culture an almost universal common denominator. Only flows in people – migration – remained highly restricted, particularly where those people were seeking to migrate from poor to rich countries.

As economic globalization gathers momentum, China and the United States have become highly interdependent economically. Such economic relations would not enjoy sustained, rapid growth if they were not based on mutual benefit or if they failed to deliver great benefits to the United States.
Xi Jinping

Globalization would appear to be a natural result of the development of capitalism and its worldwide spread. However, one key difference, not predicted by either neoclassical or Marxist theory, is that in contrast to the 19th century, the recent flow has not mostly been of goods and capital from richer to poorer countries. Rather, there has been both growth in trade between richer countries, and, crucially, a huge rise in exports from poorer countries (above all China) to richer ones like the US, accompanied by equally large capital flows. As a result, the US now 'owes' China well over a trillion dollars in Treasury securities alone.

Globalization and inequality

Perhaps the most dramatic, and most disputed, of globalization's consequences is its impact on wages and inequality (see Chapter 42). And here, both neoclassical economics and, in one respect, Marx have performed well. As predicted, the addition of hundreds of millions of low-paid, but willing, workers from China and other countries to the global economy, combined with reductions in transport and communication costs, have led to 'factor price equalization'. That is, wages for low and semi-skilled workers in developed countries have done badly in the face of competition, while wages for workers in poor countries have risen. The result has been a sharp fall in global inequality; but significant rises in inequality within countries, especially richer ones. It has not been a good time to be a manual worker in the US or the UK.

> The 1 to 2 billion poorest in the world, who don't have food for the day, suffer from the worst disease: globalization deficiency. The way globalization is occurring could be much better, but the worst thing is not being part of it
> Hans Rosling

What next?

Did the pandemic, which led to both a sharp fall in global trade, as well as calls to 'onshore' production of vital supplies like vaccines, mean that globalization has paused or even gone into reverse? This seems unlikely. The technological and political forces driving it won't go away, and in some respects may intensify, especially when it comes

Several years ago my partner and I drank tea in a fruit orchard on the edge of the ancient city of Palmyra, in what is now Syria, and bought a bottle of pomegranate molasses – then an exotic ingredient in the West – from the owner. Today, Palmyra has been occupied and partially destroyed by Islamic State militants, who want to expel the influence of Western capitalism, and what they see as its associated cultural decadence, from the Islamic world. Meanwhile, you can now buy pomegranate molasses at my local Tesco supermarket. Such are the contradictions of cultural globalization – it expands our horizons, but at the same time the reactions it provokes are not necessarily benign.

to trade in services, as the rise of remote working illustrates. The next jobs to be threatened in developed countries may well be those of relatively skilled workers in some service industries. Equally, however, we can abandon the illusion that this progression will be smooth and painless. Global linkages mean that global crises propagate faster and have more widespread impacts. It's going to be a bumpy ride.

The condensed idea
We are all connected

35 The Chinese miracle

The global impact arising from the gradual liberalization of state control in China over the last 35 years cannot be exaggerated. On the face of it, nothing could better exemplify the transformative power of capitalism, but China's development has been very different from that of earlier capitalist transitions.

When I visited Shanghai just after my 18th birthday in 1984, the skyline was dominated by the remnants of the freewheeling capitalism of the early 20th century, when Shanghai (effectively under the colonial control of foreign powers) was one of the major financial centres of East Asia. The Bund was lined with Art Deco buildings from which you could look over to the peaceful rice fields of Pudong. Now the skyscrapers of Pudong, fully five times as high, dwarf the Bund, and Shanghai, with the world's biggest container port, is the economic centre of the world's second largest economy.

Under state control, the vast majority of the Chinese population lived in villages and worked in inefficient collective farms or factories that produced mostly shoddy goods. Almost everyone was poor, but the 'iron rice bowl' system meant that nobody starved – a marked contrast to the famines of the early years of communism resulting from the forced collectivization and industrialization of Mao Zedong's Great Leap Forward.

But since the start of market reforms in 1979, China's economy has grown by more than 9 per cent a year on average. That sounds impressive, but it's even more so when you realize it means the economy is now more than 40 times larger. Over that period, perhaps 400 million people have moved from the countryside to the cities and factories of China's west and southern coasts, and more than half a billion have been lifted out of poverty.

China is different

Despite these dramatic results, the transition to a capitalist system in China has been gradual and carefully managed by the state, itself under the control of the communist party. In the words of Deng Xiaoping, who initiated the process and led it until 1989:

'By socialism we mean a socialism that is tailored to Chinese conditions and has a specifically Chinese character. This calls for highly developed productive forces and an overwhelming abundance of material wealth.'

First agriculture was liberalized, then entrepreneurs were allowed to set up small businesses, while at the same time state-owned enterprises reduced their workforces. But there has been no free-for-all, either for labour or for capital. The movement of workers from rural to urban areas, and from large, unproductive state-owned enterprises to more productive private ones, may have been vast, but it has also been controlled. The *hukou* system of residence permits, tied to place of birth, still makes it hard for people from rural areas to move to the cities. So while Chinese cities are huge, there is relatively little of the uncontrolled migration to the city that is seen in other industrializing countries like India, Brazil or Nigeria.

Access to capital, meanwhile, remains largely under state control, with big banks still state-owned, and restrictions on inflows of foreign investment. The classical economic model of development says that

China, as a relatively poor country with ample supplies of low-cost labour, should have been running a trade deficit and attracting substantial inflows of investment during this phase of rapid development. Yet in stark contrast to these predictions, China's very high savings ratio means that it has in fact been running a large trade surplus. As a result, China has been financing investment in the US rather than vice versa. Moreover, while not exactly Keynesian in the conventional sense, China has used all the possible tools of macroeconomic management – fiscal and monetary policy, as well as control over credit via state-owned banks – to keep growth high and relatively stable. Conflicts between labour and capital are also carefully managed, with trade unions mostly under the control of the Communist Party.

China's future

So China is still far from being a 'normal' capitalist economy. One view is that the country is very much in a transitional phase: over time, capital markets will be further liberalized, and state control, both economic and perhaps political, will be reduced. Chinese households will consume more and save less, and the Chinese system will converge gradually and steadily to a normal model. The impressive record of the authorities to date in combining growth with stability should give the Chinese cause for optimism.

The rise to power of Xi Jinping, who has adopted a much more confrontational approach abroad and a much less liberal one domestically, both economically and politicallly, makes this optimistic view seem much less plausible. The pattern of development so far has accumulated huge imbalances in the system. Many enterprises have benefited from access to cheap credit, with the government loosening policy every time a downturn threatens. But this means that many of the savings of individual Chinese have been

China's history is marked by thousands of years of world-changing innovations: from the compass and gunpowder to acupuncture and the printing press. No one should be surprised that China has re-emerged as an economic superpower.

Gary Locke,
US Ambassador to China

channelled via state-owned banks or the shadow banking system into loans that may never be repaid. There will be no easy way out of this without some sort of crash, with political and economic consequences that are hard to predict.

Equally, there are question marks over whether China can escape the 'middle income trap' (see Chapter 11). So far, the two main engines of growth in China have been capital investment, and the movement of labour from country to cities. Because it had so much catching up to do, this in itself was enough. But in future, if China is to close the still-huge gap with the advanced economies, more and more growth will need to come from innovation and technological progress. No one doubts that China has the raw human resources to deliver, but the system will still have to change.

And what does this mean for the rest of the world? The trade relationship between China and the United States is the largest and most important the world has ever seen. China's exports to advanced economies have helped keep inflation low, but have also probably restrained wages, while the resulting surpluses have led to a huge global financial imbalance, with China owning more than a trillion dollars of US government debt. This further increases the level of interdependency between the world's two largest economies, so political and economic turbulence in China could potentially have significant implications for the world as a whole. China's future, both in the short and long term, matters for all of us.

The condensed idea
Economic and world history in the making

36 The land of the free?

Although capitalism was born in Britain, the United States is its spiritual home. In Britain, industrialists and the new middle class, dependent on trade and commerce, had to struggle to win economic and political power from the declining aristocracy and agricultural interests. In the US, they were the dominant political force from the start. The defeat of the slaveholding, agricultural South by the rapidly industrializing North during the US Civil War of 1861–65 was a victory for freedom, but it was also a victory for capitalism and industry. It set the stage for the United States to become by far the dominant capitalist economy over the next century and a half.

A different model

However, capitalism developed quite differently in the US to Europe. In Europe, trade unions and parties representing the interests of industrial workers had demanded both regulation of working conditions and a share of political power. So the development of capitalism in Europe in the second half of the 19th century was dominated by economic and political conflict between capital and labour (and occasional bouts of repression),

This was largely absent on the other side of the Atlantic. While trade unions and other populist anti-capitalist movements did emerge in the US, they never attained the power or reach of those in Europe. Nor did a major political party emerge to represent workers' interests (partly as a result of the ongoing legacy of slavery, which meant that until the 1960s, the Democratic Party remained hostage to Southern segregationist elements). While European ideologies such as socialism, trade unionism and anarchism did cross the Atlantic with immigrants (especially from Germany and Italy), most new arrivals saw the US as a chance to make a fresh start. The image of a land of opportunity, where everyone has a fair chance to make their fortune, was and remains very powerful.

The result is a model of capitalism that looks in many ways quite different to that of other advanced capitalist economies, especially in Europe. Workers' rights and protections are far weaker, and the rights of business owners and management to run their business as they see

The US is still the largest and most important economy in the world, but it is not the single dominant force it was for much of the post-war period. From representing over a third of the world economy, it is now less than a sixth. This doesn't mean that the US economy is shrinking – it's just grown much slower as others, especially China, have caught up.

This has huge economic and geopolitical implications, but perhaps more than that it has psychological ones. We are used to thinking of the US as the model capitalist economy, but now it is just one, albeit a very important one, among many.

US Share of Global GDP

fit correspondingly stronger. Most US workers can be dismissed at will – something that would be unthinkable in most of Europe or Japan. The social safety net is also considerably weaker: the US still does not have universal health insurance, working hours are considerably longer and paid holidays shorter.

American exceptionalism

Perhaps most importantly, strong cultural differences remain: Americans are far more likely to want to set up their own business, far more likely to believe that they have a fair chance of success, and far more likely to accept the risk of failure (and to try again if they do fail). This gives the US model considerable strengths and weaknesses. It remains very dynamic – far more so than Europe. The US and

Europe have similar numbers of very large firms, but hardly any of the European ones were founded in the last 30 years, while one in seven of the US firms were. Apple, Amazon and Facebook have no equivalents outside of the US – and indeed, their most likely challengers come from Asia.

But the flipside of US dynamism is an extraordinary concentration of wealth and power, particularly in recent years. During the current economic upswing, virtually all the proceeds of economic growth have gone to the top 1 per cent of the income distribution, while average incomes for the other 99 per cent have been flat. Successful entrepreneurs have done very well indeed, but so have many of those working in the financial industry or elsewhere in the corporate sector, whose work is much less obviously related to the economic value actually generated.

The dark side

Meanwhile, workers with fewer or no skills, or those unlucky enough to work in jobs vulnerable to automation or industries facing increased competition from trade, have suffered. The US model works very well in quickly reallocating capital from old or failing firms to new and more dynamic ones, but recently it has been rather less efficient in reallocating workers (particularly since many of the fastest growing firms, especially in the tech sector, are far less labour-intensive). Moreover, the US political system, with almost no controls on election spending, means that money translates into political power far more directly than in most countries (see Chapter 24).

> This American system of ours, call it Americanism, call it capitalism, call it what you will, gives each and every one of us a great opportunity if we only seize it with both hands and make the most of it.
>
> Al Capone

So the United States now presents something of a paradox. On the one hand, US capitalism appears to be in good health; the country remains the richest and most productive large economy in the world. US firms currently dominate the fastest-growing and most innovative industries, particularly the tech sector. But on the other, the living standards of US households have, for most, lagged far behind economic growth, and the political system has largely failed to respond. Unsurprisingly, this has led to the growth of populist movements, on both the left and (especially) the political right, from the so-called 'Tea Party' movement to Donald Trump. On the international front, while the trading relationship between the US and China is the largest the world has ever seen, and is vital to both countries' continued economic health, political tensions are growing.

The US has faced similar challenges before – at the turn of the 20th century and during the Great Depression – and in both cases succeeded in addressing them without undermining the fundamental principles of its model of capitalism. Does the political system have the capacity to respond today? And what would such a response look like – a sustained attempt to rein in the excesses of the financial sector, and spread the benefits of the wealth generated in the tech sector more widely? Or a turn inwards, with a more confrontational approach towards China, both politically and on trade, combined with more populist policies at home? The US might not dominate the world economy in the way that it did in the second half of the 20th century, but it is still capitalism's leading edge.

> So, then, to every man his chance – to every man, regardless of his birth, his shining, golden opportunity – to every man the right to live, to work, to be himself, and to become whatever thing his manhood and his vision can combine to make him – this, seeker, is the promise of America.
> Thomas Wolfe

The condensed idea
The end of US dominance

37 Consumerism

The human instinct to improve our material position is deeply rooted in our evolutionary past: command over resources, especially food and shelter, made early humans much more likely to reproduce. The same instinct is foundational to both modern economics and the way we think about capitalism. The desire to acquire income and wealth, so as to afford material goods, is what motivates individuals to work, save, invent and invest.

Adam Smith showed that these motivations benefit not just individuals themselves, but society as a whole. However, this raises an obvious question: how much is enough? The overwhelming majority of people in advanced economies (and an increasing proportion elsewhere) have more than enough income to provide for food, shelter and other material needs. This poses a potential problem for capitalism. If we can produce enough for most people to be at the point where they benefit little from greater income and more consumption (see Chapter 46), then what will motivate them? Growth would stop, and we would enter a period of economic stagnation. This wouldn't necessarily be a bad thing – indeed, it would be the direct consequence of the fact that we were sufficiently content with our material lot not to need to try to improve it further. But it would be a very different type of economy and society.

Conspicuous consumerism

Happily (or otherwise) this situation doesn't appear to be the case, at least not yet. Although – as measured by the value of the goods and services we can afford to consume – we are at least twice as rich as we were half a century ago, the urge to consume more seems no less strong. American sociologist Thorstin Veblen argued, in his *The Theory of the Leisure Class*, that conspicuous consumption was a way of signalling economic status in a stratified society. In particular, by being able to consume things that were obviously useless, or to spend time on non-productive activities, members of the economically dominant classes could show how well off they were, while the rest of society was forced, by economic necessity, to get on with the actual work.

This explanation no longer seems plausible. There is plenty of conspicuous consumption around, but our society does not value conspicuous leisure, or non-productive activity: nobody suggests that people who work in tech start-ups or investment banks don't work hard. The same is true of those who work in sectors that many would point to as representing the cutting edge of consumer capitalism, in the

> You can't always get what you want. But if you try sometimes you just might find, you get what you need.
> The Rolling Stones

sense that they make money from products and services that are clearly 'unnecessary'. Whatever you may think of Kim Kardashian, or indeed more broadly, of what she represents about modern society, she's certainly not lazy.

Keeping up with the Joneses

More recently, sociologists and psychologists have suggested that relative incomes, and presumably relative consumption, matter a lot to our perception of well-being. We compare ourselves to other people in similar situations, and measure whether we are rich or poor relative to them – 'keeping up with the Joneses'. So wherever you are in the distribution of income and wealth, you'll always think you'd be a little

Planned obsolescence

Early capitalism tried to deal with the problem of 'satiation' in part by planned obsolescence – that is, by deliberately ensuring that consumer goods didn't last too long, and had to be regularly replaced. For example, a cartel of lightbulb manufacturers, known as Phoebus, after the Greek sun god, stipulated a maximum lifetime of 1,000 hours. Today, this sort of behaviour is generally classed as criminal. However, although not the result of collusion, there's still plenty of planned obsolescence in everything from sneakers to smartphones, where advances in either technology or fashion mean that there is always pressure on consumers to get the latest model.

bit happier if you were a little bit richer. It is this that allows the UK's *Daily Telegraph* to describe a London couple earning £190,000 per year – probably in the top 0.1% of the world income distribution – thus:

> 'The pair are worried about becoming financially broken as the sheer cost of middle-class life in London means they are stretched to the brink.'

Surely a classic example of what the Twitter hashtag describes as #firstworldproblems!

Clearly, individual businesses that produce and market consumer goods and services have a strong interest in perpetuating this attitude via advertising and marketing. Only thus will it be economic to continue to produce better and better smartphones, flat-screen TVs and so on. The consumer society, then, arises largely from a combination of this natural human inclination to compare ourselves with others, and the powerful economic forces of capitalism that incentivize businesses to take advantage of that instinct.

Limits to consumerism

So are there any upper limits to consumption? Physically, yes. There is a limit to how much we can or should eat, how big a house most people are likely to want, how many cars a household can actually use, and so on. And patterns of consumption will eventually have to change: if

Luxury goods

To see conspicuous consumption in action, one only has to look at a picture of superyachts in Monaco, or the 'How to Spend It' pages of the *Financial Times* weekend magazine. Items such as hand-painted handbags costing thousands of pounds, watches endorsed by superstar footballers and televisions with increasingly implausible resolutions are obviously of very high quality, but their attraction goes well beyond that: they are primarily a means for the owners to display their exceptional wealth and taste.

everyone on the planet consumed similar quantities of fossil fuels or meat as the average American (or created as much waste), we would indeed all be in trouble. Consumer societies in China and India will have to look rather different to the US today – less dependent on fossil fuels as an energy source, producing less waste and recycling more.

This is already happening to some extent: TVs, computers and smartphones are generally lighter and occupy less physical space than 20 years ago, but huge amounts of money and effort are invested in producing newer models that are even better – that is, more desirable to us as consumers. And the explosion of products and choice is even greater in services that don't themselves consume physical resources, such as entertainment and communications. Over time, we should expect more and more of our consumption to be of things that have little or no direct physical impact (see Chapter 48).

This may be more sustainable environmentally, but it's still consumption. Those who don't like the excesses of consumerism might hope that as our material needs are satisfied and as manufactured goods get cheaper, relative to a greater variety of services, we'll worry less and less about keeping up with the Joneses and more about our own life satisfaction and enjoyment of non-material things. It's equally possible, of course, that we'll just spend more time keeping up with the Kardashians.

The condensed idea
We all want just a little bit more

38 Unemployment

I f capitalism is so great, and if Adam Smith's invisible hand ensures that resources are put to their best possible use, then why are people unemployed? In 2015, more than 200 million people, some 6 per cent of the global workforce, wanted a job but couldn't find one. What better indication could there be that capitalism is inherently flawed?

Unemployment often means poverty and deprivation for individuals and families, while at the same time representing a waste of economic potential for society as a whole. So it's little wonder that its causes and cures are one of the topics that most divides economists. There are at least three competing explanations for why unemployment exists:

• **The purist free-market view** is that people are only unemployed out of choice or because of state intervention. There is a market for labour, and a price at which supply equals demand; so if the person who wishes to supply labour is willing to lower their price enough, then someone will hire them. But if the state intervenes by providing benefits to the unemployed, then some people will choose to be unemployed rather than work for little or no extra money. The Victorian Poor Law system was based on this view. Those who couldn't or wouldn't support themselves through work were forced into workhouses, which, in the words of the utilitarian philosopher Jeremy Bentham, should be the 'objects of a wholesome horror' – in other words, they were supposed to be so unpleasant that any alternative would be preferable.

• **The Marxist view**, meanwhile, is that capitalism both causes and requires unemployment. The capitalist mode of production gives owners an incentive to reduce costs, while capital accumulation allows them to invest in labour-saving machinery. This means that capital is always substituting for and displacing labour, creating unemployment (Marx's 'reserve army of the unemployed') and at the same time keeping wages down and profits up. This in turn allows the expansion of new industries. Unemployment is therefore inevitable, and only under an entirely new system could work be guaranteed for all.

• **The Keynesian view** is that unemployment represents a shortage of aggregate demand. If markets worked perfectly, prices would adjust to bring supply and demand into balance. So when demand and the price of goods fell, so too would wages. But Keynes hypothesized that in the short term, prices for both goods and labour would be slow to adjust. Instead, the burden would fall on output and employment, resulting

> Unemployment is like a headache or a high temperature – unpleasant and exhausting but not carrying in itself any explanation of its cause.
> William Beveridge

in involuntary unemployment. Government intervention, through fiscal or monetary policy, was required to restore full employment.

None of these explanations, however, is entirely convincing. Even under the Poor Laws, with wages being determined in largely unregulated markets, unemployment fluctuated considerably. And the Great Depression, when unemployment in many countries not only rose to unprecedented levels but stayed there for the best part of

The return of unemployment in Europe

In contrast to the United States, unemployment was high in many European countries throughout the 1980s and 1990s. But in the 2000s, it fell steadily, and just before the 2008–9 recession, it had fallen below 7 per cent. During this crisis, unemployment shot up in both the US and Europe. It has since fallen back to pre-crisis levels in the US, UK and Germany – but in France, Italy, Spain and Greece it remains at rates ranging from 10 per cent to 25 per cent, with youth unemployment still higher. Does this represent structural problems with the functioning of those countries' labour markets, or is it the inevitable result of failed austerity? I think both are responsible, but in any case the economic and human waste this represents ought to be unacceptable – and the unrest it causes poses a threat to the future of the European Union.

a decade, convinced most that supply and demand did not automatically balance. Marx's view that unemployment would keep pay permanently depressed seemed to have been comprehensively disproved by the steady rise in wages throughout the 20th century. After the Second World War, Keynesian demand management did maintain unemployment at historically low and stable levels for 30 years, but despite this, unemployment began to creep up again from the 1960s in most industrialized countries, especially in Western Europe.

> There should be no unemployment. There is a large percentage of labour now which cannot make a living because wages are not high enough. That is industry's second job. Its first job is to make a good product. Its second is to pay a good wage.
>
> Henry Ford

But each of these theories also has an element of truth. While few people choose to subsist on unemployment benefits (which are hardly generous in rich countries, let alone in poor ones) it is not heartless to suggest that at some level benefits can discourage work, or that minimum wages set at too high a level may keep some relatively low-productivity workers out of jobs. Innovation and technological progress are a necessary feature of capitalism, but they do destroy jobs and put people out of work, if only temporarily. And there is no doubt at all that Keynes was right about the importance of demand, as the 2008–9 financial crisis and its aftermath have made clear.

Frictional, structural and cyclical unemployment

The current conventional wisdom is to analyse unemployment as a combination of three factors. Firstly, there is always some level of frictional unemployment, as jobs are destroyed, and displaced workers have to spend some time looking for new opportunities. But, secondly, there is also structural unemployment, resulting from the way that labour and other markets function, or fail to do so. Structural unemployment could result from benefits being 'too generous', although there isn't much evidence of that in most countries. More likely, it is the result of some potential workers not having the skills they need, of discrimination keeping people out of the labour market, or of hiring and firing rules that make it too risky for employers to take on workers. All of these factors inhibit the 'job-matching' process that puts job seekers together with potential employers. Together, structural and frictional unemployment make up what is usually called the NAIRU, or 'non-accelerating inflation rate of unemployment'. This is the equilibrium level of unemployment, or the level consistent with stable inflation. On top of this there is cyclical unemployment, resulting from a deficiency in aggregate demand.

Can we solve unemployment?
The good news is that we should be able to address the unemployment problem, or at least its most damaging manifestations. Marx was right that capitalism does mean a constant cycle of job destruction and creation, but the impacts of this are more benign than he thought. There may even be a role for government in positively encouraging frictional unemployment by providing benefits that allow workers to give up jobs and search for new ones better suited to their talents. Structural unemployment, on the other hand, is not a given: it can be reduced by measures that make the labour market work better, from ensuring education systems provide people with useful skills, to public employment services that help match employers with jobseekers. And finally, while demand management on its own is not enough, it certainly has a vital role to play in dealing with cyclical unemployment: the huge rises in unemployment in many European countries over the last decade show what happens when governments forget the lessons of Keynes.

The condensed idea
A mostly unnecessary waste of human potential

39 Culture

When we talk about British or Japanese culture, we mean the ideas, customs and social behaviour of a particular people or society. But if most or all modern societies are defined to a large extent by how the economy functions, is there a 'culture' of capitalism? Both Marx and Keynes thought that a combination of benign government (communism for Marx, and managed capitalism for Keynes) and economic progress would lead to a flowering of culture. We would be able to satisfy our material needs with relatively little time and effort, and this would allow us to devote the rest of our time to higher pursuits – music, art, poetry and so on – without financial motivation.

The culture of capitalism – and the business of culture

It hasn't quite worked out that way. Instead, culture and entertainment, in the broadest sense, are two of the most fiercely competitive and globalized businesses. This applies to both high culture, as represented by the international art market, and popular culture, like football or popular music – although the boundaries are often increasingly blurred. Capitalism has indeed enabled us to spend more time both producing and consuming cultural products, but the imperatives of capitalism mean that these are just as much products, to be bought and sold in the market, as more tangible items.

As with other goods and services, the dynamism of the market has meant an explosion in the amount and variety of both high and low culture. More writing, more music, and more art are produced now than ever before. Technology means that we have access to some of the greatest works of art and literature in history at the touch of a button – as well as an astonishing amount of rubbish.

But, as in other spheres, capitalism has a tendency to concentrate wealth and power. Because many cultural products require a large investment in marketing and distribution, but are easy to duplicate at low cost, they have some of the features of a natural monopoly. For example, the global film and music industries are dominated by a few very large US companies (although there are thriving local industries in some larger countries, such as India).

Gramsci and cultural hegemony

Is culture in modern capitalist societies specifically 'capitalist'? Antonio Gramsci, an Italian communist of the first half of the 20th century, argued that the cultural norms of society are not ideologically neutral, but are (implicitly or explicitly) imposed by the ruling class. Political and economic dominance, or 'hegemony', is reinforced by cultural dominance. And certainly it does appear that contemporary capitalism has a very specific culture – English-speaking and largely produced in the US. This means that some cultural phenomena, such as *Star Wars* and Manchester United football team, can become global in a way that has never before been the case.

It could be argued that this common culture is benign, promoting understanding between the peoples of different countries – the 'universal language of football', for example. But more often, it is criticized for imposing, via the market, a standardized, dumbed-down version of US culture at the expense of older and more local ones. McDonald's and Starbucks replace fish and chip shops and pubs in Britain; the popularity of mass-market American films in English means that French-language cinema is no longer viable. And, as

A Hollywood parable

The epicentre of capitalist culture in the 20th century was of course Hollywood. In their 2016 film *Hail, Caesar!* the Coen Brothers celebrate (mostly) Hollywood's 1950s' Golden Age through the eyes of studio manager Eddie Mannix (Josh Brolin). In the main storyline his leading actor (George Clooney) has been kidnapped by a group of communist screenwriters, upset at their exploitation by the studio system. Meanwhile, Mannix manipulates the lives of directors, stars and gossip columnists, treated primarily as cogs in the machine. All this is done in the service of an unseen but all-powerful boss, and all (as the communists point out) in order to cement both the economic dominance of the studio and the ideological dominance of capitalism itself. At the end, Mannix rejects an easier and better-paid job with the darker side of capitalism – the military-industrial complex – in order to continue with 'God's work' in the movies.

Gramsci argued, the dominant American culture certainly has a strongly pro-capitalist message embedded within it. Whether deliberately or otherwise, it's embodied in everything from Andy Warhol's Pop art (based on the new technologies of mass production) to the entrepreneurial self-empowerment of Beyoncé and Taylor Swift. Indeed, successful popular musicians are near-perfect examples of contemporary capitalism at work.

Does this matter? After all, consumers are presumably choosing to eat in McDonald's, listen to Beyoncé and watch American films in preference to the alternatives. For some it clearly does. The pathology of Islamic State militants in Syria and Iraq is as much a reaction to American cultural imperialism (with its messages of individualism, female empowerment and the abandonment of supposedly outmoded cultural norms such as the more conservative interpretations of Islam) as it is to military or political events. Although far more extreme, intolerant and violent, this gives it a passing resemblance to the attitudes of some in the US itself over issues like gay marriage and abortion, which are often seen as part of an agenda pushed by a liberal, capitalist elite in Hollywood and New York.

> Hegemony operates culturally and ideologically through the institutions of civil society which characterize mature liberal-democratic, capitalist societies. These institutions include education, the family, the church, the mass media, popular culture, etc.
>
> Dominic Strinati

Meanwhile on the left, it is argued that capitalism is so embedded in the way we think about society – which owes more than ever to what we see and read – that any genuinely radical alternative is, quite literally, unthinkable. If there are no plausible representations of societies where markets are not the main way that resources are allocated, or where the profit motive is not central to a functioning economy, it is very difficult to conceive of a society that is anything other than capitalist.

So capitalist culture is certainly not morally neutral: it is part of the wider economic system, and helps to maintain and perpetuate it. But what is the alternative? Keynes' vision that growth would allow culture to somehow float above, and separate from, the mundane business of producing material goods and services now seems naïve. But so too does Gramsci's hope that the creation of an autonomous working-class culture would lead, in time, to the overthrow of capitalism. Economic growth may mean that culture becomes a steadily more important part of our lives, but as long as we live in a predominantly capitalist economy, the imperatives of profit will mean that culture is shaped by the market. And as in other spheres, creative destruction (see Chapter 10) will mean that culture continually evolves, perhaps at a pace that is too fast for some of us.

The culture of capitalism is devoted to encouraging the production and sale of commodities. For capitalists, the culture encourages the accumulation of profit; for labourers, it encourages the accumulation of wages; for consumers, it encourages the accumulation of goods. In other words, capitalism defines sets of people who, behaving according to a set of learned rules, act as they must act.
Richard Robbins

The condensed idea
Capitalism is universal
and so is culture

40 Evolution

The 19th century was a time of unprecedented scientific as well as economic progress, and undoubtedly the discovery with the most profound social and cultural implications was evolution. Just as Karl Marx changed the way we thought about how economic forces determine the structure of society, so Charles Darwin changed the way we thought about the natural processes that gave rise to humanity.

The theory of natural selection states that individuals with certain characteristics are more likely to survive and hence reproduce and (to the extent that these characteristics can be inherited) pass them on to the next generation. This has obvious parallels in the way that successful businesses in a market economy survive and grow, while less successful ones fail or are taken over. As Darwin explained it:

> 'Can it, then, be thought improbable ... that other variations useful in some way to each being in the great and complex battle of life, should sometimes occur in the course of thousands of generations? If such do occur, can we doubt (remembering that many more individuals are born than can possibly survive) that individuals having any advantage, however slight, over others, would have the best chance of surviving and procreating their kind? On the other hand, we may feel sure that any variation in the least degree injurious would be rigidly destroyed. This preservation of favourable variations and the rejection of injurious variations I shall call Natural Selection.'

Darwin and Marx

Marx was not slow to recognize the parallels between Darwin's work and his own. He saw Darwin as providing an intellectual underpinning to his theory of class struggle and the progression of history from capitalism to communism. But actual capitalists, unsurprisingly, took a rather different approach. If the 'survival of the fittest' principle in evolution was valid, then anything that interfered with it might benefit individual members of the species, but would presumably be bad for the species as a whole. Similarly, in capitalism, anything that constrained competition (harsh though it might be for workers and less efficient competitors) must be bad for the economy and society as a whole. As industrialist Andrew Carnegie put it:

> 'The law of competition, be it benign or not, is here; we cannot evade it; no substitutes for it have been found; and while the law may be sometimes hard for the individual, it is best for the race, because it ensures the survival of the fittest in every department.'

Oil magnate John D. Rockefeller similarly compared the 'growth of a large business' (and at its peak his was by far the largest the world had ever seen) to the 'working out of a law of nature'.

But the direct analogy between capitalism and evolution only goes so far. The mechanisms by which companies succeed are quite different from those by which species evolve. In particular, evolution works via random mutations. Some of these, but by no means all, are beneficial, in the sense of making the organism more likely to survive and reproduce; they therefore become more common in the next generation. But the survival of firms is due to how well they adapt to market conditions, and this in turn is due to decisions made by people managing or working in the firm, which are very much not random.

> Darwin has interested us in the history of Nature's Technology ... Does not the history of the productive organs of man, of organs that are the material basis of all social organization, deserve equal attention?
>
> Karl Marx

Social Darwinism

The application of Darwinian theory to social processes was also taken up by darker forces. Some adherents of 'social Darwinism' argued that civilization, by protecting the weak and enabling them to survive, inhibited human evolution. This view was rejected by Darwin himself, who emphasized the importance of cooperation for species, like humans, that live in groups.

However, this line of thought led ultimately to eugenics, the view that we could improve the species as a whole by ensuring that weaker individuals and groups did not reproduce. It was also used to justify racism: although there was no scientific basis for the view, white Europeans naturally saw themselves as higher on the evolutionary scale than Africans and Asians. And this in turn provided a convenient justification for imperialism: if indigenous populations could not withstand the economic and military power of European states, they were clearly unfit to survive. The eventual association of this view with Nazism effectively discredited it, and after the Second World War most natural scientists were keen to emphasize that evolution was a scientific theory about how species evolved, with no necessary implications for human society.

Evolutionary economics

But while eugenics and its association with racial superiority remain taboo, 'evolutionary economics', the application of principles from evolutionary theory to thinking about how economies develop, has become fashionable again in recent years. Much conventional economic modelling assumes that efficiency is driven by how 'rational' economic agents maximize their welfare, subject to some fixed constraints – that is, they take the external environment as given. By contrast, evolutionary economics focuses on 'adaptive efficiency', or how economic agents adapt to changing circumstances. This builds on Joseph Schumpeter's theory of creative destruction – that economic progress is driven not only by individual firms maximizing profits, but also by less successful ones failing while more successful or innovative ones thrive (see Chapter 10). Moreover, the characteristics that make firms succeed (which could be anything from an innovative product to a particular management approach) propagate throughout the system.

This approach is also potentially useful for thinking about the way economies actually evolve in practice. Like economies, species and ecosystems don't evolve smoothly; there are episodes of far more rapid change and indeed 'mass extinctions', while there can be booms and busts in the populations of individual species. These phenomena can all be observed in economics as well. More sophisticated views of evolution that are now mainstream in biology, recognizing the

Darwin's moths

One of the most famous early examples used to illustrate
Darwin's theory was directly inspired by the Industrial Revolution.
The peppered moth is mostly white, but a frequent mutation
turns it black. Before the Industrial Revolution, the black ones
were quickly spotted by birds and eaten; but after soot from
Manchester's mills changed the colour of the trees on which
they lived, being black became an advantage, and that became
their dominant colour. Following the Clean Air Act of 1956, the
process reversed. This simple example illustrates two concepts,
both relevant to how businesses and economies work. First,
the importance of context: neither white nor black is objectively
better, it depends on the broader environment. And second, the
advantages of adaptability – mostly, the mutations are usually for
the worse for the individual moth, but overall, the fact that they
occur enabled the species as a whole to survive.

importance of cooperation and even altruism as well as competition
between individuals and small groups, are also relevant to economics.

Particularly since the 2008–9 financial crisis, there has been
increased interest in using approaches that can reproduce crises in
economic modelling. Will Darwin's theories help us decide how much
the government should raise taxes, or predict the next crash? Almost
certainly not. But a capitalist economy is not just a market or set of
markets – like the natural world, it is a constantly changing ecosystem.

The condensed idea
Survival of the fittest

41 Greed

How much is enough? At what point does the desire to make more money in order to live in comfort become greed? And does it matter? Textbook economics suggests that the richer you are, the less you should care about making more money – a concept known as 'diminishing marginal utility'. And measures of happiness or well-being generally seem to confirm this.

According to most studies, a general rule is that if you're poor, an extra $10,000 will make you a lot happier, but if you're already rich, it won't make that much difference. So if this really is the case, why not put up the top rate of tax to 80 or 90 per cent, and redistribute the money, thereby making the poor better off without hurting the happiness of the rich much, if at all? Or perhaps we could levy a very large wealth tax, or set a maximum salary? For precisely these reasons, Anthony Atkinson, the world's leading expert on the measurement of inequality, thinks we should put the top rate of income tax up to at least 70 per cent, while Thomas Piketty, author of *Capital in the 21st Century*, argues for a global wealth tax on top of that.

In practice, however, most advanced economies do nothing of the sort – and indeed the trend has been in the other direction. The problem seems to be that whether or not it makes them happier, and whether or not they 'need' it, people who are already rich do indeed want to get still richer. Investment bankers who earn a million dollars a year want to run hedge funds for $10 million a year. Baseball players in the US with average salaries in the millions go on strike to extract more money from the billionaires who own the teams. And so on.

Would business leaders, entrepreneurs or even footballers work less hard for their success, and create less wealth, if the rewards were smaller or more limited? In some respects, probably not. There is relatively little evidence to suggest that 'performance-related pay' (all too often not actually related to performance in any meaningful way) means that senior executives do a better job. Neither is there much sign that overall corporate performance has improved at the same time as the ratio of a chief executive's pay to that of the average workers in a US company has gone from 20 to 1 (in 1965) to more than 300 to 1 today. And while highly paid sports stars are undoubtedly exceptional, highly motivated and talented individuals, they were likely little different some 50 years ago when they were paid far less.

Just a way of keeping score

But in other respects, it seems likely that getting richer does matter – Microsoft, Google and Facebook compete intensely, not because their founders and owners have any 'need' for more money, but because the sort of person who puts all their time and effort into founding a successful start-up is also the sort of person who wants it to grow bigger and bigger. And it's not just about companies that are already big. There are hundreds of entrepreneurs in technology start-ups working 70 or 80 hours a week in the remote but not impossible hope that they might be the next Facebook.

> The world says: 'You have needs – satisfy them. You have as much right as the rich and the mighty. Don't hesitate to satisfy your needs; indeed, expand your needs and demand more.' This is the worldly doctrine of today. And they believe that this is freedom. The result for the rich is isolation and suicide, for the poor, envy and murder.
>
> Fyodor Dostoyevsky,
> *The Brothers Karamazov*

In this context, money is not an end in itself – in the words of US oil billionaire H.L. Hunt (at one point supposedly the richest man in the world, and the basis for the character of J.R. Ewing in the TV series *Dallas*) it's simply a way of keeping score. And we all know that, regardless of whether or not there's any actual prize for winning, games without a scoring system just aren't as interesting, and motivate us much less.

It can also be argued that the desire of the rich to grow richer both creates wealth and generates tax revenue for the rest of us. And crucially, even though many of us might find the underlying motivation here questionable, or even incomprehensible, there is little doubt that we do indeed benefit. There may be plenty to worry about in the activities of a Google or a Facebook, but overall, both the wave of technological innovation we have seen over the last 20 years, and the continuing competition to come up with still further advances, are good for consumers.

The happiness equation

Money can't buy you happiness? Well, actually, it can. There is now a large body of economic research that looks at happiness, life satisfaction or well-being surveys, and tries to work out whether people who are better off are indeed happier. Broadly, the answer is yes: countries with higher average incomes report higher average levels of happiness, and within countries, people with higher incomes report being more satisfied.

But money definitely isn't everything. In general, the richer you are, the more money you need to feel even happier, as the chart here shows. Note the scale, which shows that each time you double your income, your life satisfaction will increase by roughly the same amount – moving from an income of $10,000 to $20,000 has the same impact as moving from $50,000 to $100,000.

Above a fairly moderate level of income, other things – notably relationships, health and a reasonably satisfying job – matter considerably more. If you're not actually poor, then it seems that love does trump money. All this suggests that while it's reasonable for governments to worry about economic growth, unemployment and poverty, as individuals, if we're in a decent job, our salary should be fairly low down the list of priorities.

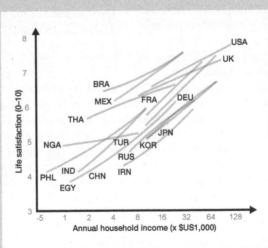

In other words, even if conventional economics can't explain it, and psychology suggests it may be actively damaging for some, contemporary capitalism benefits from the existence and efforts of a small set of people who are highly motivated by (for want of a better word) greed. Moreover, if we're lucky, maybe some of the billionaires will feel obligated to give some of their money back to society, just as the 'robber baron' capitalists of the late 19th century, such as Rockefeller, Carnegie and Frick, did in their own time.

The rich are different from us.
F. Scott Fitzgerald

Yes, they have more money.
Ernest Hemingway

A need for greed?

So what would we do if we wanted to limit or abolish 'greed', while at the same time retaining the dynamism of a capitalist economy? Higher taxes, or restrictions on executive pay, might well do less damage than many think; companies would still be able to recruit chief executives, and the European Champions' League would play on. In the financial sector, in particular, it is not at all obvious that restricting the outsized financial rewards on offer would do the wider economy any harm at all – quite possibly the opposite.

But competition, and the desire to 'win', do seem to be fundamental to both the good and bad sides of capitalism. We could, if we collectively chose, make being greedy both less socially acceptable and much more economically difficult. But there would surely be a price.

The condensed idea
Greed may not be good, but it's not all bad

42 Inequality

All societies are unequal, but some are more unequal than others. Marx argued that capitalism would lead to ever-increasing inequality, as a greater and greater proportion of the economy's output was captured by a small class of capitalists who owned and controlled the means of production, but is that really inevitable?

The late 19th and early 20th centuries did indeed see a period when inequality, as measured by the share of income or wealth going to the top 1 per cent or top 10 per cent, rose substantially. But not only did this trend stop, it was sharply reversed. In the US, the era of 'robber-baron' capitalism, when a few men used their monopoly positions in strategic industries to extract huge profits with little or no competition, was brought to an end by government intervention. Inherited fortunes, often dating to the pre-industrial era, were eroded by taxes and inflation, with some destroyed completely by the Great Depression. Most of all, the post-war welfare state redistributed income and wealth within the basic framework of a capitalist economy.

The return of inequality

But inequality rose again after the mid-1970s. Unemployment increased as the successes of Keynesian economics gave rise to 'stagflation' – a combination of rising prices and low growth. Led by Thatcher and Reagan, the welfare state was cut back (although not eliminated). Tax and social security systems did less to close the gap between rich and poor, while a less regulated economy and the reduction of union power meant that wage differentials between higher earners and the less well-off rose.

Deeper forces were also at work. Changes to production processes, and the increased importance of skills, meant that the wage premium received by well-educated workers, or those with specific skills, increased. The growth in inequality was the market economy at work: highly skilled workers were worth more to employers and were rewarded accordingly. Direct attempts to reduce wage inequality would damage the economy: so if you were worried about the social implications, the obvious remedy was to improve the education and training system so that workers were better able to compete.

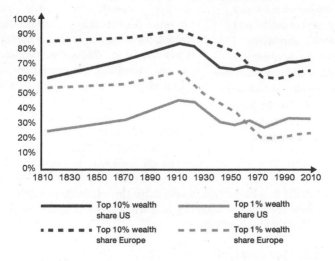

Wealth inequality in the US and Europe

Legend:
— Top 10% wealth share US
····· Top 10% wealth share Europe
— Top 1% wealth share US
- - - Top 1% wealth share Europe

But recently a challenge has emerged to this view. In his *Capital in the 21st Century*, French economist Thomas Piketty argues that it was the post-war period that was exceptional, with fast growth driven by technological change, a growing labour force and political circumstances that favoured redistribution. In the long run, he suggests we are heading back to a situation where capital is both increasingly concentrated in a few hands, and takes a growing share of the overall economic pie.

There are two central parts to Piketty's argument. The first is that the return on capital invested (and hence on wealth) is, and will continue to be, higher than the rate of economic growth. Indeed, critics claimed that his book could be summed up by the single equation: $r > g$ (the return on capital is greater than growth). This means that capital and the income derived from it will, over time, grow faster than labour income.

> The greatest country ... is not that which has the most capitalists, monopolists, immense grabbings, vast fortunes ... but the land in which there are the most homesteads, freeholds — where wealth does not show such contrasts high and low ...
> Walt Whitman

> When the rate of return on capital exceeds the rate of growth of output and income ... capitalism automatically generates arbitrary and unsustainable inequalities that radically undermine the meritocratic values on which democratic societies are based.
>
> Thomas Piketty

The second plank of the argument is that ownership of capital will become increasingly concentrated among the richest in society – the top 1 per cent or so. This will in turn lead to an increasing concentration of political power in the hands of the wealthy, further slowing growth and inhibiting political action to redistribute income or wealth.

Both Piketty's theories and the empirical evidence he advances to support them have been hotly disputed. But he'd be the first to admit that there is nothing inevitable about these predictions; what happens will depend crucially on how political institutions respond.

A global perspective

But perhaps the most important criticism of Piketty's argument is that his is purely a developed-nation perspective. Looking at the world as a whole, a very different picture emerges. The real story of the last quarter century has been the rise of a global 'middle class' – not middle class in the American or European sense of the word, but rather people in emerging economies who are not in poverty, but have incomes of perhaps up to $5,000 a year. At the same time, lower income groups in richer countries have done very badly. This reflects the greater opportunities open to the former resulting from the integration of their countries into the global economic system, but also perhaps the greater competition that the latter have in turn been exposed to. In a sense, this too is a modernized version of a Marxist concept – the 'reserve army of the unemployed' holding down workers' wages here on a global scale, and to the advantage of the owners of capital, who have also done very well (it would be surprising if the top 0.1 per cent, and especially the top 0.01 per cent, hadn't done considerably better than even the graph on page 169 suggests).

This sheds rather a different light on the evolution of inequality, at least from a global perspective. Should we worry about inequality within countries, or that of the world as a whole? And how much does

Is inequality good for growth?

If everyone is equal, there is no incentive to work or to invest. Arthur Okun, an American economist, summed up the conventional wisdom that there was a trade-off between 'equity' and 'efficiency'. High tax rates to finance higher social benefits, for example, will reduce inequality but may also discourage effort and hence reduce growth. But recently this conventional wisdom has been challenged. Hardly anyone thinks total equality is either feasible or desirable, but there are lots of reasons why too much inequality might damage growth. Poor people might suffer ill health, or not be able to afford to educate their children. Both would damage productivity. If inequality leads to higher debt, this could increase financial instability. If wealth is too concentrated, the rich may take control of the political process and use it to preserve their own power and wealth, resulting in economic stagnation. There is an increasing consensus that, at some level, inequality is harmful, and that some redistribution is not only socially just, but also economically efficient.

an increasing concentration of income and wealth among a very small number of people in some rich countries matter, both politically and economically, compared to the rapid income growth for large numbers in emerging economies?

What seems clear is that growing inequality is not an inevitable consequence of capitalism. And moreover, too much inequality could do serious economic damage. The question is whether our political systems, both national and global, are up to the challenge.

The condensed idea
Inequality is about politics as well as economics

43 Poverty

The poor will always be with us, Jesus said. But both levels of poverty and the way we define it have changed considerably across time and between countries.

By any standards, even those of the time, poverty was high in pre-industrial societies. Large numbers of people lived at or below subsistence levels, most engaged in agricultural labour. Meanwhile, a relatively small number of people were relatively very well off, either because they owned land or because they were able to extract the surplus from those who worked on it. And that's even without taking account of serfdom and slavery, which were prevalent across most of the world most of the time.

Compared to this, capitalism and industrialization expanded economic opportunities for the mass of the rural population. During the first Industrial Revolution in Britain in the 18th and 19th centuries, people moved to the towns to work in factories. They often earned low wages and sometimes lived in terrible conditions, but they did it voluntarily, because it was still preferable in material terms to remaining in rural areas.

That experience has been repeated in many countries ever since. We often focus on the very real poverty and deprivation seen in urban slums, but people move to them for a reason, usually that conditions are far worse in the villages from which they have come: the slums at least offer work and opportunity. For example, Bangladesh's textile industry is notorious for sweatshops where workers, mostly women from rural areas, are exploited and mistreated. And even well-run textile factories that avoid the worst abuses don't exactly pay well by Western standards. But the fact is that, in general, both economic and social opportunities are far better for Bangladeshi women in factories than in rural areas. Indeed, overall poverty in Bangladesh has declined substantially over the last decade, in large part as a direct result of the increased earning opportunities available in the textile industry. Moreover, there are positive feedback effects. When women have greater opportunities to earn and to participate in the economy, they are less likely to marry early and will probably have fewer and better educated children, all of which will help reduce poverty in the future.

Poverty has fallen

This progress has been seen in most of the world. The proportion of the world's population who live in absolute poverty (defined as less than $1.25 a day) has fallen sharply over the last 30 years, particularly in China, where industrialization has progressed rapidly. Most extremely poor people now live in sub-Saharan Africa and India, the majority in rural areas untouched by industrialization and where capitalism has yet to make an impact. These statistics seem to back up the claim that 'capitalism is the greatest economic system for poverty reduction'. But why, then, does poverty persist in advanced capitalist economies? Countries like the US and UK produce more than is necessary to ensure that all our citizens have enough to meet their material wants. This increase in overall income was foreseen by Keynes, and he concluded therefore that we would not have to worry about poverty or deprivation, since there would be more than enough to go around:

> The only cases in which the masses have escaped from... grinding poverty... are where they have had capitalism and largely free trade. If you want to know where the masses are worse off, worst off, it's exactly in the kinds of societies that depart from that.
> Milton Friedman

'Thus for the first time since his creation man will be faced with his real, his permanent problem how to use his freedom from pressing economic cares, how to occupy the leisure, which science and compound interest will have won for him, to live wisely and agreeably and well.'

But even rich countries still have poor people

But it hasn't worked out that way. While absolute poverty is almost entirely absent in developed countries, it is generally accepted that poverty is not just about having enough money to survive, but depends on time and place. One general definition is that poverty is about having enough income to participate in society in a meaningful way. (Keynes would probably have agreed.) And neither have the worst manifestations of poverty been eliminated even in the richest countries. Hundreds of thousands of people in the UK visited foodbanks in 2015, mostly because they could not afford to eat.

Relative and absolute poverty

In practice, we think of poverty in rich countries as a relative concept. In other words, it is not so much about starving or being below the basic level of subsistence, but about having much less than the average person. The standard definition of poverty in most advanced countries is an income of less than 60 per cent of the median. There is plenty of evidence that poverty, defined this way, both reduces people's abilities to participate fully in society and diminishes their opportunities and life chances – and those of their children. By this measure, poverty, while it fell in the post-war period, is not falling now, and indeed has recently risen in many countries.

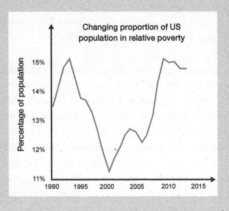

It's not too difficult to find explanations for this. Poverty, and its absence, is not just about how much we produce, but about how income and wealth are distributed – and these in turn depend on the economic and political structures that are in place. Poverty fell sharply in almost all developed countries after the Second World War with the establishment of welfare states, social security and pension systems; at the same time, near full employment (for men) and strong unions meant that wages for low and middle income earners grew sharply.

But there was nothing about the economic structure of capitalism that made this inevitable; all these changes were the result of the post-war political settlement, and over the past 30 years, many of them have largely been reversed. It is noticeable that poverty has grown in countries where these reversals have been most marked, like the US and UK, as well as those that have been worst hit by the last economic crisis in Europe, such as Greece and Spain.

So we have a paradox. On the one hand, capitalism is indeed the best, and perhaps the only, way for the vast mass of people in developing countries to escape poverty. But a rising tide does not lift all boats. Capitalism will not, on its own, ensure that everyone has the economic wherewithal to participate in society. To do that we need an additional set of institutions: economic, social and political. Developing countries need health and welfare systems that protect those who lose out as nations get richer. And all countries need political and economic structures that ensure that wealthy elites do not capture all the benefits of growth. We have made a huge amount of progress in the past few decades, and there is absolutely no scientific or technological reason why we should not end poverty entirely – but it won't happen automatically.

> Poverty entails fear, and stress, and sometimes depression; it means a thousand petty humiliations and hardships. Climbing out of poverty by your own efforts, that is indeed something on which to pride yourself, but poverty itself is romanticized only by fools.
> J.K. Rowling

The condensed idea
We can end poverty – if we choose to

44 Immigration

Human beings have been moving in search of economic opportunities since they migrated out of Africa 100,000 years ago. But it was only the invention of the nation-state and the creation of borders that defined 'immigration' as a separate economic and political phenomenon. And in many countries today, immigration is perhaps the most visible and politically controversial aspect of our globalized economy.

The essence of the economic case for migration is very simple, and it's the same as the case for free markets in general. If people take decisions on the basis of their own economic self-interest, this will maximize overall welfare. This applies to where people live and work just as much, if not more, than it applies to buying and selling goods and services. Of course, markets fail, and 'more market' is not always better. But the view that, as a general proposition, markets are good at allocating resources (including human resources) is widely shared among economists.

This analogy holds in a narrower, more technical sense as well. The classic argument for free trade, as advanced by Adam Smith, is not just analogous to, but formally identical to, the argument for free movement. In economic terms, allowing somebody to come to your country and trade with you (or work for you, or employ you) is very similar to removing trade barriers with their country. Certainly, it's grossly hypocritical for politicians who claim to be in favour of free markets or free trade to then turn around and argue for increased restrictions on immigration.

But just as with trade, that does not mean everyone wins from an increase in immigration. Most of the gains, of course, will go to the immigrants themselves. And some people (especially workers who are in direct competition with immigrants) will lose out, at least in the short term. Marx argued that capitalism required a 'reserve army of the unemployed' to ensure that workers could not demand higher wages. For some, immigrants serve the same function.

For these reasons, the trade union movement in advanced economies has historically had a somewhat conflicted relationship with immigration. This has sometimes even been tinged with racism, since non-white (or indeed southern European) immigrants were thought particularly likely to be prepared to work for low wages. The Australian trade union movement and Labor Party, for example, supported the 'white Australia' policy throughout the first half of the 20th century.

But the view that immigrants simply take jobs that could be done by native workers, known to economists as the 'lump of labour' fallacy, is flat wrong. By virtue of having a job and earning money (which they then spend), immigrants create demand for goods and services, and hence for more labour, just as they add to the supply of labour themselves. Over time, these impacts even out.

> The rapidly developing industrial countries ... raise wages at home above the average rate and thus attract workers from the backward countries. There can be no doubt that dire poverty alone compels people to abandon their native land, and that the capitalists exploit the immigrant workers in the most shameless manner. But only reactionaries can shut their eyes to the progressive significance of this modern migration of nations.
> Lenin

Indeed, it is surprisingly difficult to find evidence that immigrants push down wages for native workers by much, or reduce their employment prospects at all. Several studies in the UK have failed to find any significant impact from high levels of recent immigration on native employment. Even quite large influxes of refugees, such as those to Israel in the 1990s, or to Turkey in recent years, seem to have a surprisingly small effect.

Immigrants bring dynamism

What does seem to be true is that immigration makes countries more dynamic and productive. Immigration seems to be associated with increased innovation, international trade and knowledge transfer, particularly in high-tech industries. Speaking personally, I work in a sector (economic research in London) where many, perhaps most, workers are originally from elsewhere. While that means I face more competition, it also makes the sector as a whole larger and more efficient – and probably also raises my income over time.

Immigrants are also more likely to be self-employed, and may be more entrepreneurial – perhaps because more enterprising people are more likely to move countries in search of opportunity, or because it is harder for immigrants to get jobs at large companies or in the conventional labour market. And of course some of the most successful large companies of recent times, such as Apple and Google, were founded by people with immigrant backgrounds.

But what about the countries from which the immigrants come, especially developing countries that may be losing skilled and educated workers? Perhaps surprisingly, they don't seem to lose out either – instead, they seem to gain as much from money sent home by immigrants and the resulting increases in trade. It appears, for example, that immigration from India to the US has both been good for Silicon Valley in California, and for the growing Indian IT industry in Bangalore.

The influx of foreign workers holds down salaries, keeps unemployment high and makes it difficult for poor and working class Americans to earn a middle class wage.

Donald Trump

But immigration has wider social impacts as well. In the aftermath of the 2008–9 financial crisis and the ensuing recession, there has been considerable political reaction against immigration in the US and in many European countries. From an economic point of view, these concerns are almost certainly misdirected. That is, immigration, like trade, is not the main cause of stagnating wages or reduced employment prospects, so reducing it will not make those who suffer economically any better off. From a political point of view, however, attacking immigration is easier than calling for policies that might, for example, require higher taxes or difficult reforms.

Immigration is an opportunity

What does seem clear is that the political, environmental and economic pressures that have led to increased immigration in recent years (wars in the Middle East, drought and high population growth in sub-Saharan Africa and so on) are, if anything, likely to intensify. Properly managed migration has the potential to both hugely benefit the migrants themselves, and be an opportunity for receiving nations, particularly those in Europe that face declining populations. But to make this work, countries will have to manage integration better than some have done in the past – which is a political challenge at least as much as an economic one.

> As an immigrant, I chose to live in America because it is one of the freest and most vibrant nations in the world. And as an immigrant, I feel an obligation to speak up for immigration policies that will keep America the most economically robust, creative and freedom-loving nation in the world.
> Rupert Murdoch

The condensed idea
Free markets should mean free movement

45 Stagnation

Since the financial crisis of 2008–9, most advanced economies have seen a painfully slow recovery, with growth remaining well below the levels before the crisis, and unemployment still high in many countries, especially in Europe. Is this no more than a temporary blip, from which we will naturally recover? Or will growth continue to stagnate? A prominent economist, Alvin Hansen, once foresaw that the world might be entering a new era of long-term reduced growth:

> 'This is the essence of secular stagnation – sick recoveries which die in their infancy and depressions which feed on themselves and leave a hard and seemingly immovable core of unemployment.'

Hansen was writing in 1938, just as rearmament was about to restore both fast growth and full employment in the US and elsewhere. After the war, the steady and stable growth made possible by Keynesian economics (which Hansen did much to popularize in the US) left the 'secular stagnation' concept largely forgotten. And even after Keynesian macroeconomic management went out of fashion, the view remained that if governments and central banks ensured economic stability, growth and employment would follow almost automatically.

Recovery, what recovery?

However, the post-2009 period has thrown that view into doubt. In contrast to recoveries from previous post-war recessions, where output and productivity grew fast, recent productivity in the G7 group of large advanced economies has grown by less than 1 per cent a year on average; in the UK and Italy it has hardly grown at all. Former US Treasury Secretary Larry Summers revived the concept of secular stagnation in 2013, arguing 'the presumption that normal economic and policy conditions will return at some point cannot be maintained'.

But what could explain the persistent failure of to return to 'normality'? Essentially, there are two separate issues. The first is the hypothesis that we are just entering a period where growth is naturally lower. Hansen suggested that this might be because of demographic

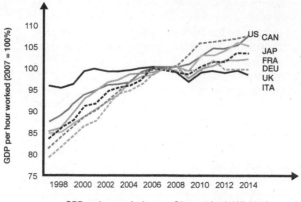

GDP per hour worked across G7 countries (1997–2014)

changes and slower population growth. He was wrong at the time, but the thesis looks more plausible now. In Germany and Japan, the working-age population has been shrinking for a decade, and (despite immigration) growth is slowing elsewhere – even in the US and UK. It has also been argued that productivity growth will naturally slow: much of the very fast growth in the decades after the war reflected an unusual combination of circumstances (rapid technological progress, a sharp rise in average educational attainment and favourable demographics).

But this argument seems difficult to maintain. For most of us, it seems as if technological progress is far from slowing down. And more broadly if this were the case, then productivity should have been declining gradually and gently: this argument doesn't explain what suddenly changed in 2008–9.

It's the demand, stupid

The second half of the secular stagnation thesis is about demand. Proponents point to interest rates, which, even after the post-pandemic rise in inflation, remain low by historical standards. At the end of quantitative easing in most advanced economies, demand for safe, long-term government bonds remains very strong, while private investment demand is weak. In other words, markets are signalling that lots of firms and people want to save, and few want to invest,

particularly in the sort of risky investments that generate future
growth. Instead, they're choosing to put their money in low-risk, low-
yield government bonds.

The usual policy prescription for this classic Keynesian problem
would be to cut interest rates – and that is what we tried in the run up
to the pandemic, with little success. Summers' argument was that the
equilibrium level of long-term interest rates, at which growth and
employment would return to 'normal' levels, has fallen. It may even
have dropped below zero, at least in real terms – real rates are still
negative, and this could mean that we get stuck in a prolonged period
of low growth and low rates.

If the problem is, indeed, lack of demand, then the government
should be able to do something about it. But what? Ultra-low interest
rates appear to have been unsuccessful in spurring productive
investment, but may have resulted in asset price bubbles – increases in
the cost of housing, stocks and other financial assets that are not
justified by their underlying value. This may have supported demand
in the short term, by making people feel richer, but sooner or later the
music will stop, and there will be another crash.

Time to borrow and spend
The obvious alternative is to use fiscal policy, in which government
soaks up the excess savings by borrowing and spending more,

especially on investment in infrastructure. Many economists – myself included, but increasingly also major international institutions such as the International Monetary Fund and the Organization for Economic Cooperation and Development – have been arguing that this makes sense, almost regardless of your views on Keynesian approaches to macroeconomic policy or the desirable size of the state.

At a time when interest rates on government bonds are still at, or below, zero in real terms, private investors are essentially offering to pay governments to take money off their hands, so it seems crazy not to take them up on this offer (particularly given the obvious need for higher spending on things like road and rail networks in countries such as the US, Germany and the UK).

But politicians, having seen borrowing soar during the last 20 years, are reluctant to borrow still more. In both the Eurozone and the UK, an unfortunate reaction has been for governments to sign up to arbitrary restrictions on their borrowing that made little sense even in normal times, and are positively damaging now. If private investment demand is likely to remain low for some time, then reducing government investment and pursuing a budget surplus is not just unnecessary but actively harmful. Similarly in the US, political gridlock makes getting a consensus on higher spending nearly impossible. Genuine political and economic vision would be required to change this, and that seems in short supply just now.

The condensed idea
The end of economic growth

46 Abundance and superabundance

Economics is sometimes defined as the study of the 'allocation of scarce resources'. But what happens – not just to economics, but to economies and societies – when resources are no longer scarce? Technological progress means that we are least five times as productive as we were a century ago.

Before long, we may be confronting the situation first set out by Keynes in 1930, when the industrialized world was mired in the Great Depression. Capitalism was in crisis, and in time, Keynes would both explain the origins of the crisis and how an activist economic policy could save capitalism before it destroyed itself. But before that, he wanted to raise his readers' sights above the immediate, and point out that over the long term economic growth would not only make us richer, but inconceivably wealthy by historical standards:

> 'This is only a temporary phase of maladjustment. All this means in the long run that mankind is solving its economic problem. I would predict that the standard of life in progressive countries one hundred years hence will be between four and eight times as high as it is today.'

In the decades since, Keynes has been proved right, and if anything, economies have grown even faster than he anticipated.

Prosperity is recent

For most of history, the vast majority of people lived not far above subsistence levels, often no more than one failed harvest away from famine. Today, the vast majority living in advanced economies are unimaginably prosperous in material terms. While it may seem premature, even callous, to talk of abundance in a world with nearly a billion people living in abject poverty, that number has been shrinking steadily, and from an economic and technological point of view, there does not seem to be any reason why it should not continue to dwindle.

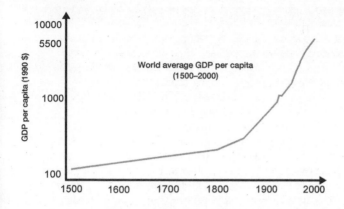

GDP per capita (1990 $)

World average GDP per capita
(1500–2000)

If anything, the speed of progress is accelerating. Advances in technologies such as 3-D printing, nanotechnology and robotics mean that it is now more plausible to suggest that we will, as Keynes suggests, 'solve the economic problem', in the sense that we will be able to produce enough for everybody on the planet to have all the material goods they want or need. In the last 40 years, US manufacturing output more than doubled, while the number of workers halved. Increasingly, little or no direct human input will be required: for example, at the Great Wall Motors plant in Tianjin, China, robots can weld together an entire car in a minute and a half.

The end of capitalism?

But what will this mean for the economy and society? Keynes was hopeful. He foresaw the end of capitalism, in the sense that the profit motive would not only cease to become the driving force for progress, but would be regarded as positively abnormal:

> 'All kinds of social customs and economic practices, affecting the distribution of wealth and of economic rewards and penalties, which we now maintain at all costs, however distasteful and unjust they may be in themselves, because they are tremendously useful in promoting the accumulation of capital, we shall then be free, at last, to discard.'

What would a post-capitalist society look like? The most plausible vision is perhaps like that of *Star Trek*, a world where food and material goods are produced by replicators, bodies can be quickly repaired or even replaced, and the entire corpus of human knowledge and culture is available at the touch of a button. With recent advances in 3-D printers, organs being grown in laboratories, the Internet and smartphones, none of this now seems out of our grasp (although interstellar space flight remains a long way off). So what do people in *Star Trek* actually do? Some are explorers, boldly seeking out new worlds; but it appears that most of those who remain on Earth do more or less what Keynes expected, which is to pursue well-being, but not profit, through the peaceful cultivation of arts and culture, philosophy and other such occupations. Even Captain Picard eventually retires to grow grapes somewhere in France!

Instead, we would spend our time seeking 'to live wisely and agreeably and well.' Capitalism would, through its own success, have destroyed itself.

But despite our material advances, from a societal point of view this vision seems further off than ever, even in the richest countries. For better or worse, it is still the profit motive that drives technological progress. There is no evidence at all that when societies become much richer, people are less motivated by the pursuit of wealth. And while we are certainly far better off in material terms than in Keynes' time, relatively few of us can afford not to work full-time for a living.

Or ever increasing polarization?

Instead, many fear that automation and mechanization will lead to huge riches only for a very few – those who either invent or commercialize new discoveries, or who inherit wealth. A relatively privileged class whose skills remain valuable will enjoy prosperity and comfort, but for a large (and perhaps growing) number who simply have little to offer economically, the result will be unemployment and marginalization. As long as income remains distributed primarily on the basis of the individual's market value, few will be able to take advantage of the theoretical attractions of abundance.

One possible way out that has lately become increasingly popular among economists is the idea of replacing the existing welfare state (which insures against unemployment, poverty and old age, but assumes fundamentally that people can and should work most of the time) with a 'basic income' or 'social dividend'. That is, we should provide everyone with the means to pay for the necessities of life, and individuals could then choose whether to work or not, to write poetry or to invent new gadgets.

> In a sufficiently prosperous society where people specialize sufficiently, and where enough of the crappy work is done by machines, all work becomes art.
> Nick Hanauer,
> US businessman

This would represent a profound social transformation, away from a society that assumes you have no automatic right to resources unless you at least try to contribute, to one where abundance means that expectation is no longer necessary, and people can 'contribute' in any way they choose. Would this destroy capitalism, by making idleness an acceptable lifestyle choice, or save it, by preserving work and the profit motive for those who choose it, but ensuring some degree of social fairness in an economy that would otherwise become more and more 'winner-takes-all'? Would it be politically sustainable?

The challenge of material abundance is, from a historical perspective, definitely a good one for humanity to have. But we don't yet know how to take full advantage of the opportunities that it offers. A basic income, or something like it, may be part of the answer. But perhaps even more important will be rethinking how we evaluate the 'worth' of people in a society where there is more than enough to go around.

The condensed idea
The profit motive still drives progress

47 The future of work

Will the robots take all our jobs? We live in an era of increasing mechanization (of physical and manual work, from factories to supermarket checkouts) and computerization (from call centres to tax returns). But does this make it harder for humans, especially those with less in the way of skills or qualifications, to do anything cheaper than a machine can do it?

Economists like to point out that while new technologies do indeed destroy jobs, they do not, over the medium to long term, reduce employment. That is, while people do lose their jobs if they are made uneconomic by new technology, over time the economy as a whole adjusts, and new jobs are created. And since labour productivity ends up higher as a result (since increasing productivity is what labour-saving technology *does*), overall we become more prosperous.

So far, automation hasn't destroyed jobs

And indeed economic history shows precisely that. In 1841, more than one in five British workers laboured in agriculture; today, it is only one in a hundred. More than one in three worked in manufacturing; today it is fewer than one in ten. And of course despite those falls in the number of workers, we produce far more than we did then. Meanwhile, those jobs have been replaced. About 90 per cent of workers are now employed in service industries, and a higher proportion of the population is now in employment than at any time in recorded economic history. The fact that we can produce more food and manufactured products with far fewer people means that we are far richer overall, as the rest of us do other things, from economic research to performance art to professional football – all of which, at least on paper, contribute to overall economic output.

So does that mean we should not be worried about the threat to jobs from technological progress? Self-driving vehicles could eliminate millions of jobs in the transport sector, while barcode scanners and online shopping could do the same in retail. Recent research suggested that about half of all jobs in the US (and probably in most advanced economies) are vulnerable to automation or computerization in the next two decades. While low-skilled jobs are

The Luddites

Before the invention of spinning frames and power looms, self-employed weavers (mostly in north-west England), made a relatively good living. But new technology made their jobs obsolete. The Luddite movement protested, often violently, against mechanization of their industry, and was eventually, and also violently, suppressed. Since then 'Luddite' has become a derogatory term used against those who oppose labour-saving technologies or indeed progress more generally. However, Andy Haldane, chief economist at the Bank of England recently asked whether, two centuries on, the Luddites were going to be finally proved right: 'The space remaining for uniquely human skills could shrink further. If these visions were to be realized, however futuristic this sounds, the labour market patterns of the past three centuries would shift to warp speed. If the option of skilling up is no longer available, this increases the risk of large scale un- or under-employment.'

the most vulnerable, more complex ones are also increasingly at risk, as software becomes more capable of dealing with analytical tasks such as translating between languages, or even making basic medical diagnoses.

So as you read this, take a moment to think: what would it take for a robot, or a computer, to do all or most of what you do at work on an average day? Then think about current advances in artificial intelligence, robotics, 3-D printing, virtual reality, and make a realistic assessment of how much of your work could be automated in the foreseeable future, and how long that is likely to take.

> Everyone can enjoy a life of luxurious leisure if the machine-produced wealth is shared, or most people can end up miserably poor if the machine-owners successfully lobby against wealth redistribution. So far, the trend seems to be toward the second option, with technology driving ever-increasing inequality.
> Stephen Hawking

Don't panic ... yet

Conventional economics, and history, would suggest that while these changes will be painful for some, the economy in general will adjust, and over the longer term society as a whole will benefit. If machines can perform tasks currently done by people more quickly and more efficiently, we'll all be richer.

But could things be different this time? Some economists and commentators are concerned that it might be, and they tend to focus on two main worries. First, that the pace of change is so fast, and the range of jobs that can potentially be done by machines so wide, that adjustment will simply be impossible. So far, however, there is little evidence of this – more than 4 million people get a new job in the UK every year, and in the US it's 5 million every month. Not all of these jobs are great by any means, but it does suggest that labour markets are able to cope with a rapid pace of change.

Advantage capital?

Perhaps more serious, however, is the possibility that the current wave of automation will mean a permanent shift in the balance of power between capital and labour, with social consequences that are difficult to foresee. Companies such as Google and Apple create a huge, and growing, proportion of overall economic output, at least as conventionally measured. That's not new in itself – 50 years ago, companies like General Motors did the same. But the modern tech giants employ far fewer people; GM employed 600,000 people in 1979, while Google's total staff numbers only 60,000. Although GM was, of course, heavily dependent on automation and capital investment, much of the value added went to its workforce. This is much less true of technology firms, where it is capital, often in the form of software, that does most of the work and hence gets most of the reward. And of course the software itself doesn't get paid – it's the owners of capital who benefit.

So the risk is that automation will shift the balance of power between capital and labour permanently in favour of the former. We'd move to a society where the owners of capital control the means of production and reap the rewards. Workers would probably still work, but many, perhaps most, would be in relatively low-value, peripheral jobs – not central to the functioning of the economy, and not particularly well paid. Either the distribution of income and especially wealth would widen even further, or society would rely still more on welfare payments and charity to reduce unacceptable disparities (most probably, a mixture of both).

This is a pretty dismal prospect, but it's important to bear in mind that these broader economic forces pushing against the interests of workers won't, on their own, determine the course of history. The Luddites were doomed to failure, but their successors – trade unionists seeking to improve working conditions, and Chartists demanding the vote so they could restructure the economy and the state – mostly succeeded. The real test, then, will be whether our political and social institutions are up to the challenge.

The condensed idea
Don't fear the robots

48 The digital economy

The sheer scale and scope of technological advance, driven by information technology, is difficult for most of us to comprehend. I have access both to more information and more computing power in my pocket than almost any human in existence did on the day I first started work! No one knows the economic and social consequences of these changes, but clearly they will be fundamental to the future development of our economy.

As a result of this computing revolution, governments, business-people, economists and commentators today all talk about the huge importance of the 'digital' or 'information' economy. But what is it? When we talk about the digital economy or businesses, many people think about Silicon Valley in California, or Bangalore in India. Alternatively, they might mention large multinational companies that rely on information technology hardware, software or both, like Apple or Amazon. These definitions cover the companies that produce information and communication technology products, but a wider one might also include digital content, or digital products, in everything from e-commerce to music to architecture.

Digital is everywhere

But none of this quite captures what we mean. There are of course now very few businesses (or indeed few forms of economic activity) where information technology does not figure in some form or other. In advanced countries, we all use e-mail and work for organizations that have websites. In developing countries, access may be harder for some, but the actual technologies may be even more important, from mobile banking in Africa to biometric identification in India. More fundamentally, most traditional companies – in sectors from pharmaceuticals to finance to extractive industries – rely increasingly on information technology-based initiatives to improve performance.

So the digital economy is not so much about specific industries and types of output, or certain types of firms like tech start-ups, but a complete technological transformation in how the economy works. Looking at this broader concept, what is different about the digital economy and how does it change things?

The first difference is a simple physical one – an increasingly information-based economy means one that is far less reliant on physical things. Almost 20 years ago, Alan Greenspan, then chairman of the US Federal Reserve, pointed out that output was much less closely related to physical size or weight than it used to be. This changes the nature of production and consumption. It means far fewer large factories, and far more people sitting tapping away at keyboards. It also means more people consuming the resulting output via information processing and storage devices. And it also changes the nature of trade – while a majority of commerce still requires physical goods to be shipped in containers by road and sea, more and more is simply a transfer of data of one sort or another. Indeed, in 2016, the UK became the first large economy to export more 'services' (everything from insurance to TV programmes) than manufactured goods. This matters because it means that growth in future will be much less about how we extract natural resources, process raw materials or ship products around the world, and much more about how we process data and then 'consume' the results, in industries from healthcare to entertainment.

> New developments in machine intelligence will make us far, far smarter as a result, for everyone on the planet. It's because our smart phones are basically supercomputers.
> Eric Schmidt

The second difference is the speed of change: it's not just an illusion that technological change (and in particular the speed with which a scientific breakthrough or innovative new product is widely adopted) is happening faster now. It took 40 years for half of Americans to get a landline telephone: but only 10 years for the same proportion to get a cellphone. Africa, meanwhile, never really got landlines for the vast majority of its population, but when mobiles arrived, it took only a few years for them to reach the poorest and most remote villages.

The third difference relates to economic winners and losers. One clear set of winners are the 'superstars' of culture and entertainment. Great artists and performers have always been valued, but physical constraints on their audience limited their earning power. Now, however, they can be seen (and marketed and paid) worldwide. So the most successful sportsmen and women and musicians have far greater

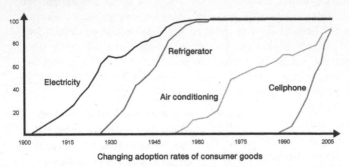

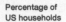

Percentage of
US households

Refrigerator

Electricity

Air conditioning

Cellphone

100
80
60
40
20

1900   1915   1930   1945   1960   1975   1990   2005

Changing adoption rates of consumer goods

economic clout than they used to, while second or third rank ones have less. Does this matter to the rest of us? Perhaps not much yet, but imagine if the same phenomenon extended to teachers, for example – and there is nothing in principle to stop one teacher lecturing a million students at once.

> In the new world it's not the big fish that eats the small fish, it's the fast fish that eats the slow fish.
> Klaus Schwab

What about winners and losers in terms of companies? Again, the fact that information can be quickly reproduced and transmitted means that the speed of change is quicker. The winners can do very well indeed, but their success may not last long. Google and Facebook, Apple and Amazon may now appear to dominate large parts of the information economy, with almost incomprehensibly huge profits and near-monopoly positions in a number of markets. But on the other hand, Yahoo and Myspace found their apparently advantageous positions were quickly eroded when better, or simply better marketed, products came along.

This is just the beginning

What is certain is that we are nowhere near the end, and perhaps just at the beginning, of the resulting changes. Just as the Industrial Revolution transformed not only the economy, but also politics and society in the space of a century, so the digital revolution is likely to

It has been estimated that ten times as much data has been produced and stored in the last five years as in the entire history of the world before that date. At the moment, the vast majority of that data is not processed or used in any economically meaningful way. But as both storage and processing capacity continue to expand rapidly, that will change. The economic pressures on firms will become more and more powerful, and consequently more and more ingenuity will be devoted to finding ways to make use of that data. This applies in particular to data on the individual actions and preferences of consumers, collected from everything we do or say online (which increasingly means pretty much everything).

do the same, perhaps much faster. This could generate huge increases not only in wealth, but also in well-being, while avoiding the damaging environmental

You have zero privacy anyway. Get over it.
Scott McNealy, Sun Microsystems

consequences that growth based on physical goods required. But it might also mean a much more brutal, winner-take-all world than either companies or workers have been used to for most of the past 70 years, with greater concentrations of wealth and power. The future is exciting, but also frankly rather terrifying.

The condensed idea
More information, less stuff

49 The environment

The economic possibilities of capitalism appear to be boundless – at least according to most economic models and to philosophers of capitalism from Marx to Schumpeter. Yet surely our planet, and its resources, are finite? In the late 18th century, Thomas Malthus argued that this must inevitably constrain population growth (and, implicitly, economic growth).

Malthus believed that the natural tendency of population would be to grow exponentially, while agricultural production would grow at most linearly. But in fact, the mechanization of agriculture, the improvements in farming technology known as the 'Green Revolution', and more recent advances have meant that food production has outpaced population growth. The world now produces about 2,700 calories per capita per day – more than enough to feed us all with plenty left over. In general, people do not go hungry because there is not enough food to go around, but because they cannot afford to buy it (see Chapter 43).

Limits to growth

But Malthus's arguments were repeated and extended to resources more generally in a 1972 report by influential think tank, the Club of Rome. The Limits to Growth predicted that continued exponential growth would mean the planet would eventually exhaust a number of finite resources, including oil.

Their argument is now regarded as widely discredited, however, because it largely ignored how the economy would actually respond to rising prices for scarce resources. Perhaps surprisingly, although we've burned through a lot of oil since 1972, we've actually got more of it left (in terms of proven reserves) than we had then. Intermittent periods of very high prices led to more exploration, as well as encouraging technological progress and the adoption of substitutes. And the same is true for other natural resources. In general, economic growth has become less energy and resource intensive, especially in advanced economies: the UK actually consumes less energy than in 1970, although it has 10 million more people and its economy has doubled in size.

But even if finite supplies of raw materials are not a constraint, what about the wider environmental consequences of capitalism? Does economic development inevitably mean environmental damage? In fact, what appears to have happened for many countries is that there has been a hump-shaped curve. As countries develop, pollution and other forms of environmental damage do indeed increase as a result of urbanization and the growth of industry. But later on, as countries get richer, they can afford to regulate more and invest in reducing pollution, and political pressures mean that they will do just that.

> **The Stone Age did not end because we ran out of stones.**
> Sheikh Zaki Yamani, Saudi Oil Minister

The city of London offers a classic example. In the early 19th century, most sewage flowed directly into the River Thames, resulting in regular cholera epidemics. Following the 'Great Stink' of 1856, Parliament authorized a massive programme of public investment to create a modern sewerage system. Smog, mostly produced by burning coal, was responsible for tens of thousands of deaths in the 19th and

Slow ... but inexorable

Exponential growth does not necessarily mean fast! Growth of 1 per cent a year is exponential; the point is that compounding means that even a slow percentage rate of growth will overtake a straight line, or linear, projection in the end.

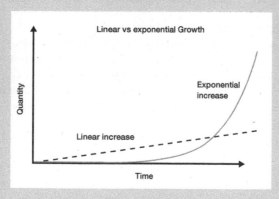

Linear vs exponential Growth

Quantity

Exponential increase

Linear increase

Time

early 20th centuries (the origin of London's still common, but now thankfully obsolete nickname, 'The Big Smoke'). Air pollution in Delhi and Beijing is equally bad today, but could (and hopefully will) be solved by tighter controls on factories, vehicles and household fuel. None of these solutions is particularly difficult technologically; they simply require money and political will.

Some argue that environmental progress in rich countries has been bought at the cost of exporting environmental degradation to poorer countries, but this logic is difficult to sustain. Pollution in Beijing comes from cars, coal-fired power plants and nearby dirty factories, but the products we import from China are mostly produced in more modern, less polluting factories to the south and east. There are horrific examples (for example, the mining of coltan in Congo for mobile phones), but these reflect state failure and corruption, and consequent opportunities for exploitation by foreign companies, rather than the economics themselves. That is not to deny that the Western companies involved, and ultimately we as consumers, have a responsibility here, but it is fundamentally a political problem.

> The science tells us that [greenhouse gas] emissions are an externality; in other words, our emissions affect the lives of others. When people do not pay for the consequences of their actions we have market failure. This is the greatest market failure the world has seen.
>
> Lord Nicholas Stern

Climate change

If local environmental problems are soluble, then what about global ones? Naomi Klein, in *This Changes Everything: Capitalism vs. The Climate*, argued that global warming is the direct result of capitalism, and can only be solved by a radical transformation of our economic thinking: 'The really inconvenient truth is that it is not about carbon – it's about capitalism.'

This is only half right. Our current levels of carbon emissions are indeed a direct result of economic development driven by capitalism, and the resulting demand for energy. But there is nothing fundamentally capitalist about fossil fuels. Imagine that somebody tomorrow invented an inexhaustible supply of cheap energy – a safe nuclear fusion reactor, perhaps. Oil companies might go bust, but capitalism wouldn't. And while it won't happen overnight, past experience suggests that, if the incentives are there, technological change will come. The price of solar power has fallen sharply over the past 20 years, and will continue to fall – a result of capitalism at work.

But, just as with smog in London or Delhi, change won't happen automatically. Global warming is just the biggest and most dangerous example of the classic economic problem of an 'externality', where someone uses a free resource in a way that imposes a cost on others. In this case, we're all guilty, and applying some basic economic principles could be the answer. If we paid a proper price for the carbon we emit into the atmosphere (whether through a carbon tax or some other similar system then two things would happen. First, we'd use less. But second, and more importantly, the incentive for entrepreneurs and inventors to come up with viable forms of low-carbon energy production would increase.

So, if (and it is a big if) we put the right regulations and incentives in place, then Naomi Klein is wrong: capitalism can solve global warming. But also wrong are those politicians and economists, mostly in the US, who claim to be great believers in capitalism and free markets, but argue that we can't afford to do anything about global warming because a carbon tax, or similar action, would do too much economic damage. For anyone who genuinely understands how capitalism works, or looks at economic history, this is scaremongering, and 200 years after Malthus, we should know better. History has shown that humans can be remarkably inventive when confronted with technological or scientific challenges. Sometimes the defenders of capitalism are its own worst enemies.

The condensed idea
Economics can save the planet from capitalism

50 Is there an alternative?

'**W**e are all capitalists now' wrote the *Wall Street Journal* after the fall of communism. It did not mean that every country in the world was necessarily going to adopt the same economic model, only that there was no longer any serious political or philosophical challenge to capitalism as the main organizing principle of a modern economy. And for a decade and a half, that triumphalism seemed amply justified.

For much of the 1990s and early 2000s, a free-market, finance-oriented version of capitalism, with its edges smoothed off a little by 'Third Way' social democracy (see Chapter 25), was the dominant model in advanced economies. Meanwhile, the extraordinary growth of China, as it adopted market-oriented policies, seemed to point the way forward for emerging economies.

But after the 2008–9 crisis, the *Journal*'s pronouncement rings more than a little hollow. Not only did globalization and the dominance of the financial sector give us the worst crisis and recession since the Great Depression, but since then we've had slow growth and high unemployment or stagnating living standards in most advanced economies. It is also far from clear that China and other emerging market economies will be able to sustain their recent rapid growth. As a result, the political consensus behind the 1989–2007 model of capitalism is no longer secure.

No credible alternatives

But while recent years have seen explicitly anti-capitalist political movements take power in a number of countries from Venezuela to Greece, in every case they have conspicuously failed to construct a viable alternative economic model. The result has been either economic and hence political chaos, as in Venezuela, or compromise with the existing order, as in Greece or Bolivia. The US 'Occupy Wall Street' movement (with its offshoots in other Western countries) has largely fizzled out, and while populism is on the rise, from the Tea Party movement in the US to the Front National in France, most such movements do not even pretend to offer a plausible economic alternative.

Leaving political developments aside, is there any plausible alternative economic system? State ownership and control of the economy were discredited by the economic and political failure of the post-war Soviet bloc, and while the Chinese development model has been remarkably successful to date, it remains very much an economy in transition from state to private control, rather than an alternative.

The obvious alternative to both state and private ownership of the means of production is worker ownership and control. This idea has a long and distinguished pedigree, from Robert Owen in the UK in the 19th century and the founding of the cooperative movement, through various strands of anarchism and anarcho-syndicalism around the world. And there are numerous examples of successful worker-owned enterprises in advanced economies – from the Mondragon federation of worker cooperatives in the Basque region of Spain, to the John Lewis group of department stores and supermarkets in the UK. And, while not strictly cooperatives, partnerships where the founders and most senior staff have a large element of ownership and control remain common in finance, law, accountancy and consultancy.

However, most cooperatives are relatively small. They have difficulties both in securing capital to finance investment, and in scaling up their governance structures. These are, of course, precisely the barriers that capitalism was invented to overcome, through the creation of joint stock companies and bond and stock markets. Even Goldman Sachs, perhaps the most well-known and powerful financial institution to use the partnership model, 'went public' (that is, became a standard company with shareholders) when it required external capital. So worker-controlled enterprises still represent a tiny proportion of the economy as a whole – less than 1 per cent in the US, for example, and there is no real sign that they are likely to grow rapidly in the future.

> Its critics ... have seen capitalism as intrinsically unstable, full of contradictions that will lead eventually to its collapse. Its supporters see it as the best way to allocate resources and rewards. Some even hint that the democratic capitalistic society is not just a phase in the historical evolution of economic systems but its ultimate end.
>
> Raghuram Rajan, Governor, Central Bank of India

We like to look to science fiction for visions of what technological change might mean for how societies are structured. Sometimes, as in *Star Trek*, money is irrelevant because all material goods are essentially free, and humans devote themselves to exploration or other higher pursuits. But dystopian visions are rather more common. The *Alien* films suggest that the logic of capitalism will lead inevitably to humanity's self-destruction. The dominant 'Company' sees the alien species as a potential profit-making opportunity, and any existential threat it poses as secondary. Numerous authors have examined the implications of a society that is increasingly stratified genetically. In Aldous Huxley's *Brave New World*, this is rationalized both from an economic perspective (it facilitates planning) and a political one. Others, from Isaac Asimov to Philip K. Dick, have looked at both the moral and social implications of artificial intelligence. More apocalyptically, the fears of Stephen Hawking, the Nobel Prize winning physicist, and Elon Musk, founder of PayPal and Tesla Motors, about a coming 'singularity', when super-intelligent machines take over, are mirrored in the *Terminator* movies.

Change is coming

So it seems there is nothing remotely approaching a viable economic alternative to capitalism at the moment – but that does not mean one may not emerge in the next few decades. Marx's fundamental insight was that it is economics, and in particular the way we produce things, that above all determines the nature of our society. Capitalism as we now know it was the result of a profound change in the nature of production, and society as a whole, resulting from the Industrial Revolution. And today we are just at the beginning of what is likely to be an equally profound set of economic changes, based on at least three key developments. In sharp contrast to the industrial age, direct physical human input into production will be increasingly rare, as robots take over. Advances in computing power and artificial intelligence will mean that much of the analytic work humans currently do in the workplace will be carried out by machines. And finally, our growing ability to manipulate our own genes will both extend our lifespans and, increasingly, allow us to determine the characteristics and perhaps even intelligence of our offspring.

Control over 'software' – data and the way it is stored, processed and manipulated – will be more and more important, compared to physical capital, buildings and machines. Recalling Marx's key insight, that what really matters is ownership and control of the means of production, the defining characteristic of the future economy and society will be how that software is produced, owned and controlled; whether by the state, by individuals, by corporations or in some way as yet undefined.

These developments will potentially mark a profound change from the current model of capitalism. They will allow us, if we choose, to end poverty and expand both our material and intellectual horizons. But at the same time they could also push in a direction of growing inequality, with the key levers of the new economy controlled by a wealthy corporate and moneyed elite. As an optimist, both for what capitalism has achieved in the past and for what it can achieve in the future, I believe the former is more likely. But just as it wasn't the 'free market', or indeed individual capitalists, who freed the slaves, gave votes to women or created the welfare state, it will be a collective effort from us all that enables humanity to turn economic advances into social progress.

The condensed idea
Change is coming

Glossary

Capital Capital means wealth or assets that can generate a return. It can refer to either financial assets (like shares) or physical ones (like machinery)

Central bank The body responsible for overseeing the monetary system of a country. This usually includes issuing currency, overseeing monetary policy, acting as the government's bank and often supervising commercial banks.

Communism A system of social organization or government where all property (in particular capital) is held in common rather than being privately owned.

Debt Debt is an obligation by one party to pay or repay money (or sometimes other financial assets) to another.

Efficiency In economics, a term with a number of different meanings. Productive efficiency is when a given output is produced with minimum cost, while technical efficiency is when the maximum output is produced from a given set of inputs. Allocative efficiency occurs when resources are allocated in the most efficient way – that is, when welfare is maximized for a given set of resources.

Efficient markets hypothesis The theory that, in general, asset prices in financial markets fully incorporate all publicly available information.

Fiscal policy The use of the aggregate level of government spending and taxation, and hence the government's budget deficit, to influence the economy as a whole. Fiscal policy that leads to a higher deficit is generally referred to as 'expansionary' policy.

GDP Gross domestic product – the market value of all goods and services produced by an economy in a given period (usually a year).

Incorporation The process of creating an entity with a legal status different from that of its owners (such as a company), which can undertake economic actions (producing, buying, selling, borrowing) on its own account, and often has limited liability.

Inflation The rate at which the general level of prices in the economy is rising, usually expressed as an annual rate.

Interest rates How much it costs to borrow money, usually expressed as an annual rate.

Keynesianism The view that the economic performance of an economy as a whole can be improved by the active management of aggregate demand using monetary and/or fiscal policy.

Limited liability A structure for a firm where the firm's owners are not personally liable for the debts of the firm beyond the level of their initial investment.

Macroeconomics The study of the economy as a whole, looking at relationships between factors like inflation, interest rates, unemployment and growth.

Markets A market is any form of environment (which can be real or virtual) where buyers and sellers interact to trade goods, services and money.

Microeconomics The study of how individuals, households and firms make economic decisions, and in particular how economic decision makers interact in markets.

Monetarism The view that controlling and stabilizing the quantity of money circulating in the economy (or its rate of growth) should be the primary mechanism for stabilizing the economy.

Monetary policy The process by which the monetary authority (usually the central bank) controls the quantity of money in the economy and its rate of growth. Central banks usually do this by controlling the level of short-term interest rates and/or by buying and selling government bonds.

Money The officially circulating medium of exchange in an economy; money also serves as a unit of account and a store of value.

Monopoly A situation when a single economic actor (usually a company) controls all or nearly all the supply of a particular good or service, and hence can set prices without fearing that an alternative supplier will charge a lower price. Monoposy refers to the (less common) situation where there is only one buyer rather than one seller.

Opportunity cost The value forgone by using some resource for a particular purpose, rather than for the next best alternative.

Profit The difference between the amount a person or business makes by selling goods or services and the amount spent in producing them (including any wages to workers, taxes, interest on loans and any other expenses).

Property Anything that is legally owned by a person or economic entity. Property can also be held in common by a group of people, or owned by the state. The rights and privileges of property owners are defined and guaranteed by the state.

Recession A period when the economy is shrinking. A recession is often, though not always, defined as two successive quarters of negative growth.

Share A unit of ownership of a financial asset – usually a limited company or corporation. It often entitles the owner to a proportionate share of the companies' profits or dividends and a voice in appointing management.

Stagflation Stagflation refers to a situation where an economy has elevated levels of unemployment and high inflation at the same time; this was a feature of Western economies in the 1970s.

Stagnation A period of sustained low growth. 'Secular stagnation' refers to an extended period during which wider economic forces or trends mean that it is difficult or impossible for government policy to generate sustained growth.

Surplus value A concept in Marxist analysis – the difference between the value of the goods or services produced by workers and the wages they are paid.

Unemployment A person is unemployed if he or she would like to work but cannot find an appropriate job. Not everyone who is not employed is unemployed – people who are not looking for a job, for example for family reasons or because of disability, are termed 'economically inactive'.

Index

About the author

Jonathan Portes is Professor of Economics and Public Policy
at King's College, London. Previously, he was the Chief Economist
at the UK Cabinet Office, where he advised the government on
economic strategy. He has written for the *Financial Times*,
Guardian, *Telegraph* and *The Spectator*.

Greenfinch
An imprint of Quercus Editions Ltd
Carmelite House
50 Victoria Embankment
London EC4Y 0DZ
An Hachette UK company

First published in 2016
Copyright © Jonathan Portes 2016, 2023

Jonathan Portes asserted his right to be identified as the author of this Work.

Design and editorial by Pikaia Imaging

Artworks by Tim Brown

A CIP catalogue record for this book is available from the British Library

ISBN 978 1 52943 017 2
eBook ISBN 978 1 52943 018 9

10 9 8 7 6 5 4 3 2 1

Printed and bound in Great Britain by Clays Ltd, Elcograf S.p.A.